Also by Cathy Hunsberger:

Secrets Your Bridge Friends Never Tell You

Dreams:
Unlocking the Mystery

A How-To Guide that Will Change Your Life

Cathy Hunsberger

BALBOA.
PRESS
A DIVISION OF HAY HOUSE

Balboa Press books may be ordered through booksellers or by contacting:
Balboa Press
A Division of Hay House
1663 Liberty Drive
Bloomington, IN 47403
www.balboapress.com
1 (877) 407-4847

Because of the dynamic nature of the Internet, any web addresses or
links contained in this book may have changed since publication and
may no longer be valid. The views expressed in this work are solely those
of the author and do not necessarily reflect the views of the publisher,
and the publisher hereby disclaims any responsibility for them.

The author of this book does not dispense medical advice or prescribe the use
of any technique as a form of treatment for physical, emotional, or medical
problems without the advice of a physician, either directly or indirectly. The
intent of the author is only to offer information of a general nature to help
you in your quest for emotional and spiritual well-being. In the event you use
any of the information in this book for yourself, which is your constitutional
right, the author and the publisher assume no responsibility for your actions.

Any people depicted in stock imagery provided by Thinkstock are
models, and such images are being used for illustrative purposes only.
Certain stock imagery © Thinkstock.

Front cover: Kristin Krahmer
Author photo: Sandra Colleen Elliott

Printed in the United States of America.

ISBN: 978-1-4525-8383-9 (sc)
ISBN: 978-1-4525-8385-3 (hc)
ISBN: 978-1-4525-8384-6 (e)
Library of Congress Control Number: 2013918193

Balboa Press rev. date: 10/31/2013

To all inquiring dreamers with the desire that you find the answers you need, and to my past and present dream groups, with gratitude for all your hard work and inspiration.

WHAT OTHERS SAY ABOUT DREAMS

"Comprehensive and reader-friendly, *DREAMS* is an articulate synthesis of dream analysis. *DREAMS* includes a framework you can start using and applying to your dreams immediately. I love the step-by-step strategies and the insightful examples."

–Sandra Elliott, Educator and Photographer

"This book is a delight! Cathy's style is simple and conversational. It feels like we're sitting around in comfy chairs having a fascinating conversation. Cathy's guidelines for remembering and understanding dreams are very easy to follow. A clear, informative, entertaining read."

–Anne Zara, Writer, Designer, Reiki Master

"What motivates a writer? The answer may be a complex mix of "I need the $$; I need the ego gratification; I need the therapy." Not bad reasons – but the higher calling for a book is to be socially useful, and without a doubt, that's what we have here. I know that Cathy's lovely, graceful, and witty dream guide will be a beacon for all dreamers who want to know more."

-Mike Stoller, Educator, Writer, Poet. [His poem, "Kong at the Gates," won The National Library of Poetry's 1994 Grand Prize.]

"*DREAMS* is thorough, engaging, and well-written. Cathy gives us an easy-going tour of her subject - from the Ancients, to that dream that startled you awake this morning."

–Joe Hannabach, author of *Autumn Moon – Two Trees*, and of *Old Mandolins – Collected Poems*.

Table of Contents

Thank You! ....**xv**

Chapter 1 What's It All About? 1
    What are dreams? How do they work?
Chapter 2 Dreams Throughout History 7
    Are dreams a New Age thing?
Chapter 3 Famous Dreamers 13
    Documentation from the rich and famous.
Chapter 4 What In The World? 21
    Types of dreams, and what they may mean.
Chapter 5 Remember Me? 99
    How to remember your dreams, including how to
    train your brain!
Chapter 6 Your Dream Journal 117
    How to record your dreams. The necessity of
    immediate action.
Chapter 7 Putting It All Together 127
    A dream interpretation manual, just for you.
Chapter 8 Mr. Dream Man, Bring Me A Dream 181
    How to generate a specific dream for a specific
    purpose.
Chapter 9 Follow Your Dreams 189
    Use your dreams to improve your life.

Bibliography 193

Index 197

My Story

Dreams have followed me everywhere. I've been chased, I've been killed. I've had a tiger knocking at my door. I've flown above the world with exhilarating freedom. Familiar spirits from beyond have come to visit. A clear message to get with the program and stop dragging my feet was delivered, in no uncertain terms.

I did not, however, always know what these dreams meant, or how important they could be for me in my waking life. It was my move from Oregon to California that started my personal dream journey.

I was introduced to a study group where everyone kept a dream journal. These dreams were discussed and interpretations pursued. My eyes were opened. Dreams did mean something after all. They were real, they were personal, and they could change my life. From that time onward, I kept my own journal.

I also attended multiple seminars, and read as many books about dreams as I could get my hands on. I talked to my friends and family about their dreams. Everything I learned seemed to be validated by what I heard and what I experienced myself.

I found a similar group when I moved to Virginia. My journals continued. It's been more than 30 years, and I now have a collection of thick journals that provide a diary of my dream life.

When it came time to retire, I found I wanted to share my experience and knowledge with others. Everyone has a dream, but not everyone goes any further than that. I wanted all dreamers to get the most possible out of every dream.

The next step was to embark on more research, read more books and periodicals [see my Bibliography], and gather more dreams. The dream examples in this book are real, but in most cases the dreamer remains anonymous to protect his or her privacy.

My hope is that you will use the techniques in this book to enjoy and make use of your dreams because, after all, dreams are real, dreams are personal, and dreams can change your life!

Thank You
ありがとう。
TACK
grazie
Bedankt
Danke Schön
merci
MERCI
OBRIGADO
gracias
GRAZIE
Tack
תודה
Merci
bedankt
GRACIAS
THANK YOU
DANKE SCHÖN
obrigado
Gracias
Grazie
Bedankt
danke schön
شكراً
thank you
Obrigado
תודה
BEDANKT
ありがとう。
tack
Merci
gracias
Gracias
THANK YOU
TACK
GRAZIE
Danke Schön
شكراً
Grazie
OBRIGADO
TACK
merci
thank you
bedankt
תודה
MERCI
grazie
obrigado
merci
gracias
Merci
tack
תודה
bedankt
Thank You
BEDANKT
grazie
Bedankt
شكراً
THANK YOU
Danke Schön

Thank You!

No man is an island. No woman is either. Writing is a lonely, arduous business. However, it is not something you can do alone.

My gratitude for family, friends, and fellow authors is boundless. Without them not even this page would exist.

Among the editors, proofreaders, and supporters are Sandra Elliott, Mike Stoller, Joyce Neville, Anne Zara, Carol Chapman, and my dream/study group. I wish I could do more than name them, but words are what I have. Words sometimes are just not enough.

What are dreams? How do they work?

What's It All About?

"All human beings are also dream beings. Dreaming ties all mankind together." Jack Kerouac.

What *are* dreams anyway? How do they work? Do they really mean anything? What good are they to *me*?

These are questions you naturally ask as you approach the dream world. You are curious about the nighttime drama that fills one-third of your life. Dreams can't be just random entertainment, can they?

There are upwards of 7 billion people on this earth. All of these people breathe, eat – and dream. Is this a meaningless coincidence? I don't think so. You are, after all, body, mind, *and* spirit; these parts of you are intertwined and connected to form a cooperative whole. Leave one of them out and you are incomplete. The dream world speaks to your spirit. The messages it brings are clothed in symbolic language. The subconscious works to bring these messages to you when you are in a sleeping state, when your usual daytime defenses are down, when you can't ignore the information you so desperately need. It is up to you to acknowledge, remember, translate, and use these messages.

So, in answer to your original questions: Dreams are a form of communication – more on that later. They are received via your subconscious while you sleep. Yes, they do mean a lot. They bring messages about your life, relationships, career, creative efforts, and more. These messages, when acted on, can change your life.

You can learn to remember, interpret, and use your dreams. The Talmud tells us, "A dream which is not interpreted is like a letter which is not read." It's time to start opening those letters.

THE DREAM PROCESS
"Pay attention to your dreams – God's angels often speak directly to our hearts when we are asleep." Eileen Elias Freeman.

What Are Dreams?
In sleep, our waking thought processes relax; built-in censorship is dropped. The conscious mind is laid aside, and a natural bridge is formed for communication.

It's like having a cell phone with connections to your subconscious, your superconscious, your guardian angels, arch-angels, deceased loved-ones, the Christ Spirit, the Universe. You have unlimited calling, towers are never down, there are no dead spots, and the line is always clear. Best of all, there is no bill – it's all FREE!

You get advice on life, on relationships, on health. You may get a pat on the back. You may get an elbow in the ribs (usually if you're ignoring your dreams). You receive counseling, explanations, clarification, enlightenment, and advice. Your intuition and creativity are accessed and given a power boost.

This is done for you, personally, individually. It is presented on *your* cell phone, no one else's, for *your* eyes and ears only. It is available every night. To everyone. And again, it is free.

Well, almost free. You do have to dial, to listen, and to interpret the message. You then have to USE the message, the information, the knowledge. You have to WANT to use the message, the information, the knowledge.

YOU are the Dreamer

You are the architect of your dreams. You set the stage, you write the script, you direct the action. You then play every part. The dream is all for you. You watch the dream unfold as the privileged audience of one.

The dream then spills over into your waking life. You remember some parts clearly; other parts stay wrapped in fog. You feel an urgent need to write the dream down, to remember, to study, to decode the message of the play. You know the message is especially for you. You know it is important. It holds clues to events currently unfolding in your life. It can give you understanding, enlightenment, hope, insight, guidance. You want to KNOW, to use those valuable kernels of knowledge that the Universe has sent to you.

You start the process. You work with your dreams, with your subconscious, your superconscious, your guardian angels, the Universal forces. Your life begins to take on a certain glow, a strength, a purpose. You ask questions, you receive answers, you take action. Things begin to HAPPEN.

Look into this world of dreams. Learn to use this oh-so-wonderful, valuable tool that is *always* available. It is a gift. It is free of charge. All you need to do is use it.

"Dreams are nature's answering service – don't forget to pick up your messages once in a while." Sarah Crestinn.

How Do I Begin?

Now is the time. Wait no longer. Receive, digest, write down, interpret, and USE your dreams. Reinvent your world. Come alive!

"But I just can't," I hear you crying. "I never remember my dreams. And I'm so busy." Well, you just "couldn't" learn to ride a bike, to play the piano, to swim, to do fractions. But somehow, you did. You tried, you practiced, you succeeded. You perhaps did not become an Olympic swimmer, or a math major, but you did your best, and you enjoyed your efforts and the results. It's the same with dreams.

You start out small, with baby steps. Soon you have a Dream Journal that is three inches thick, full of beautiful letters from the Universe that have been sent to you, and you alone, for your personal enlightenment and development. Wow!

Once you show you are serious, the mail never stops. Need health advice? You get it. Relationship counseling? Tune right in. A new job? Your dreams will point the way.

Allow me to be your companion on this journey. I will provide tips, hints, and techniques to lead you toward the river that is your inner self, your intuitive self. That river will flow through you, become a part of you, and you will meet it in your dreams. You will begin your journey toward a fuller life.

Ready? Let's get started. You don't want to wait another minute because, after all, dreams are *real,* dreams are *personal,* and dreams *can change your life.*

Are dreams a New Age thing?

Dreams Throughout History

"History tends to repeat itself." Hegel.

If you think the current preoccupation with dreams is a "New Age" thing, think again. Historical documentation shows that dreams have been prominent in the life of mankind for at least 5,000 years.

Ancient Dream History

Fascination with dreams goes back at least as far as recorded history (approximately 3,500 BC). Dream musings are found from ancient Mesopotamia, ancient Egypt, ancient Greece. Aristotle (384-322 BC) believed dreams related to a dreamer's waking experiences. Early Christians saw dreams as a time when the body and spirit were connected.

The practice of dream incubation, or programming (asking for a dream on a particular topic/problem), was active in many ancient cultures, including those of the Egyptians, Babylonians, Phoenicians, Hebrews, and Greeks. This technique was also used by tribes of Native Americans and peoples in the Himalayas, China, and Japan. Dreamers would petition the gods for a dream that would provide answers to a particularly knotty problem. A dream might be requested for spiritual insight or personal health. The dreamer would follow a ritual, which might include the use of fasting, prayer, dancing, even drugs. He would then sleep near a sacred place or object, perhaps a temple or natural landmark associated with divine power.

The Senoi of Malaysia are thought to have arrived from southern Thailand about 4,500 years ago. The Senoi believed that dreamers should confront and conquer dream danger, advance toward dream pleasure, and achieve a positive outcome. They learned to program their dreams, to shape them by suggestion, and to work in a lucid dreaming state (which is being consciously aware, while asleep, that you are dreaming). In modern times, they still share dreams, discussing them at breakfast with the family. Later, an individual might continue this sharing process with friends or colleagues.

Ancient Dream Beliefs

Ancient Egyptians believed that dreams were communications from the gods. Dreams were so valued that Egyptians priests formulated spells to generate dreams. One known spell instructed the potential dreamer to draw the god Besa in ink on his left hand. Before going to bed, the hand was to be wrapped in black cloth. The dreamer had to maintain complete silence prior to sleeping. In addition, the dreamer had to write a petition for the dream by the light of the setting sun. The petition (or prayer) asking for a specific dream, and the silence before sleeping, are part of techniques used even today to incubate dreams.

The Greeks and Romans taught that some dreams could be genuine visions, while others were about everyday life. The soothsayer Artemidorus (2nd century AD) wrote that dreams used symbols and events that were allegorical – they expressed truths or generalizations about human existence.

The ancient Chinese were of the conviction that everyone has two souls - one connected with the body and one connected with the spirit. The spiritual soul was the one involved in dreams. Each night it left the body to communicate with other spirits, bringing back messages. The spiritual soul needed time to return to the body, so family members never woke a person abruptly. Even in modern times, in some regions of China, alarms clocks are regarded as potentially dangerous.

Prophetic dreams are frequently portrayed in the Bible, using visual metaphors, angelic messengers, and the voice of God Himself.

It seems that whatever the age or culture, humans have always recognized that dreams are real, that dreams are personal, and that dreams can change your life.

Modern Dream History
"We shall require a substantially new manner of thinking if mankind is to survive." Albert Einstein.

Sigmund Freud (1856-1939) – Freud did not come up with anything the ancients had not already theorized about or addressed, except for his fixation on sex. He managed to convince the public that dreams seem strange because they are disguised messages about sex. The messages have to be disguised, he advised, because otherwise they would frighten us. An internal censor thus rewrites our thoughts using symbols, which only highly trained psychoanalysts can clear up (for a fee of course). In fact, he had a pretty good thing going there. What a great marketing device – Sex, Sex, Sex. Who wouldn't want to discover what their dreams revealed to them about their covert thoughts on sex?

Carl Jung (1875-1961) – Freud's theoretical opponent was Swiss psychologist Carl Jung. Jung believed that dreams were natural events. He saw a dream as one's unconscious speaking in its natural language, which relies less on words and more on symbols. Some of these symbols, he believed, are universal, found in folklore and religion around the world. For example, Jung believed the circle was often a symbol of wholeness and balance, as shown in much Asian art.

Jung also believed that dreams are personal and should be interpreted by the individual (at no cost!). He felt that dreams express concrete concerns or problems and give possible solutions. Jung also thought that historical or mythical figures can best be understood as expressing some aspect of oneself. Thus, because dreams are personal, they can be used by the individual to spur insight and personal growth.

Modern Theory
Today many dream theorists echo Jung's conception of dreams as potentially creative and liberating, although they don't necessarily give a lot of credence to his "universal archetypes" – symbols with similar meanings to all dreamers. A very personal interpretation of dream symbols, according to one's own experiences and beliefs, is generally preferred.

Conclusion
So for those of you who have thought of dream work as a modern device, you can now appreciate that dreams have been a focus of mankind throughout the ages.

We come, once again, full circle, to the premise that dreams are real, dreams are personal, and dreams can change your life. This has been echoed throughout history, with variations on a theme, and using multiple techniques, but always sending the same essential message.

Sometimes we have to look back to look forward. As Shawn Purvis tells us, "The light of starry dreams can only be seen once we escape the blinding cities of disbelief."

Documentation from the rich and famous.

Famous Dreamers

"Yet it is in our idleness, in our dreams, that the submerged truth sometimes comes to the top." Virginia Woolf.

Questions?
Do you sometimes ask yourself, "Are my dreams truly real? Am I just imagining things? Is there any evidence beyond my own little world that this isn't just pie in the sky?"

It can help to know that there is a lot of evidence for the validity of the dream world, not only from your next door neighbor, but from celebrated persons in history. Here are a few reports from Presidents, famous authors, even a pro-golfer:

Abraham Lincoln
President Lincoln (1809-1865) dreamt of his own assassination.

In his dream Lincoln found himself lying in his bed in the White House, listening to a deathlike stillness, which was soon broken by the sounds of weeping in the rooms below. Leaving his bed, Lincoln wandered from room to room, unable to find who was crying. The entire White House seemed deserted, but the sound continued.

Puzzled and alarmed, the dreamer continued until he came to the East Room. With a shock, he realized he had stumbled upon a service for the dead. Before him lay a corpse wrapped in funeral

13

vestments. Soldiers stood on guard; the sobbing came from a throng of mourners gathered round. "Who," Lincoln demanded of one of the soldiers, "is dead?" "The President," the soldier answered – "killed by an assassin."

Just then the crowd's grief grew more excessive, startling Lincoln awake. For the rest of the night he could not sleep, but lay in his bed, worried and haunted by his vision.

Upon waking, Lincoln reported this dream to his closest friend and unofficial personal body guard, Ward H. Lamon, who promptly wrote it down. He also told it to his wife, who became quite distraught. Lincoln, however, was determined to go about business as usual. Less than a week later, he was dead.

Stewart Alsop
Some dreams can heal. Stewart Alsop (1914-1974), a well-known political columnist, was battling cancer. It was spreading; his chances didn't look good.

One night he dreamed he was alone at night on a train, which was about to stop at Baltimore. When it did, Alsop looked out through the door at what he presumed was the Baltimore station - deserted, dimly lit, creepily silent. As silent as death. "We won't stop here," Alsop announced loudly to whoever was in charge of the train and the dream. "Start up the train, and carry on." The next day, for the first time, Alsop's x-rays looked better. The cancer had mysteriously begun to recede. He went back to work not long after.

It seems clear the dream showed the projected end of his journey; however Alsop decided to change that destination. He made the decision to live. And so it was.

"There are mysteries," Alsop wrote later about his dream, "above all the mystery of the relationship of mind and body, that will never by explained, not by the most brilliant doctors, the wisest of scientists or philosophers."

Jack Nicklaus

Pro golfer Jack Nicklaus (1940-) was suffering through a prolonged slump. He went to sleep frustrated, agonizing over what was going wrong.

A dream showed him performing a perfect stroke, using an entirely different grip.

"When I came to the course yesterday morning," Nicklaus told a newspaper reporter, "I tried it the way I did in my dream, and it worked…I feel kind of foolish admitting it, but it really happened in a dream."

Nicklaus' scores immediately improved.

Mary Shelley

The author of *Frankenstein*, Mary Shelley (1797-1851) first glimpsed her horrific creation in a dream. In the summer of 1816, she and her husband were staying with friends at the Villa Deodati on the shores of Lake Geneva, Switzerland. After an evening exchanging ghost stories, the host suggested that each of the group write a horror story of their own. Marry Shelley went to bed and had a terrifying nightmare.

"My imagination, unbidden, possessed and guided me," she later wrote, "gifting the successive images that arose in my mind with a vividness far beyond the usual bounds of reveries…I saw the pale student of unhallowed arts kneeling beside the thing he had put together – I saw the hideous phantasm of a man stretched out, and then, on the working of some powerful engine, show signs of life, and stir with an uneasy, half-vital motion."

Upon waking, she excitedly realized she had her story. She knew, "What terrified me will terrify others; and I need only describe the spectre which had haunted my midnight pillow."

President Lyndon B. Johnson

President Johnson (1908-1973) often dreamed of the difficulties he was struggling through.

In one recurring dream, as described by biographer Doris Kearns Goodwin in *Lyndon Johnson and the American Dream*, Johnson found himself in the Executive Office building signing paperwork. He rose to go home, only to discover his leg was chained to the desk. With a sigh, he would reach for another stack of papers and begin all over again.

Another recurring nightmare possessed Johnson as the war in Vietnam intensified. In this dream, he was lying on a bed in the Red Room of the White House, unable to move or speak; his body was transformed into the paralyzed, diminished frame of another president, Woodrow Wilson. To get over this dream, Johnson would walk through the dark corridors of the White House, carrying a flashlight, until he came to the place where Wilson's portrait hung on the wall. Touching the painting, he would reassure himself that he was not the man depicted therein – the man who had been paralyzed by wartime indecision.

Another dream finally helped Johnson decide not to run for reelection. In it, he was fighting to swim across a river to the bank, but couldn't reach it. He switched directions, fighting toward the other bank, but couldn't reach that either. Johnson found himself going around in circles, which, he decided upon waking, perfectly symbolized the impossible political situation in which he had become trapped.

Robert Louis Stevenson

Stevenson (1850-1895), author of *Treasure Island* and *The Strange Case of Dr. Jekyll and Mr. Hyde*, described his dreams as populated by elflike Little People, who were better at inventing plots than he was.

"Who are the Little People?" Stevenson reports asking himself. His answer: "They are near connections of the dreamer's, beyond doubt; they share in his financial worries and have an eye to the bankbook...they have plainly learned like him to build the scheme of a considerable story in progressive order; only I think they have more talent, and one thing is beyond doubt, they can tell him a story piece by piece, like a serial, and keep him all the while in ignorance of where they aim. Who are they, then? And who is the dreamer?"

We know, of course, Stevenson's unbridled subconscious was guiding his conscious self, allowing his creativity to run unchecked.

Samuel Taylor Coleridge

Coleridge (1772-1834), a major poet, in his preface to *Kubla Khan*, explained that he had fallen asleep at his farmhouse while reading a book about the Mongol emperor. Having nodded off, he began dreaming.

In his dream Coleridge began composing beautiful poetry without effort. He composed two or three hundred lines in this manner, the images rising before his eyes and translating themselves directly into words. Upon awakening, he eagerly found pen and ink and began at once to transcribe the wonderful things he had dreamed.

Unfortunately, someone knocked on the door, a "person on business from Porlock," who kept Coleridge occupied for more than an hour. On returning to the epic he had begun, Coleridge was dismayed to find that, aside from the fifty-four lines he had set down before being interrupted, it was all gone. He couldn't remember a thing.

Dream memory doesn't last long. The beauty of the 54 lines that did survive makes one ache that the remainder was forgotten. Had Coleridge known what you and I now know (or will learn shortly), he would never have answered that door.

The Rest of Us
You can see the kinds of dreams the rich and famous have. Let's look at the types of dreams that you, and I, and the rest of the world experience. They're not so different!

Types of dreams, and what they may mean.

What In The World?

"Variety's the very spice of life that gives it all its flavour." William Cowper.

Am I odd? Strange? Just plain weird? My dreams are sometimes so bizarre!

Such thoughts may cloud your mind as you pore over your dream journal (where you faithfully record your dreams each morning). Rest assured. At this very moment thousands of dreamers are having a host of dreams, many of which are odd, strange, and just plain weird. The dreams, that is, not the dreamers...

According to a survey by Henry Allen, *Washington Post*, July 7, 1982, dream frequency is as follows:

Falling – 71%
A loved one in danger or dead – 59%
Being chased and attacked – 56%
Sexual experiences – 54%
Accomplishing something great – 52%
Floating (flying) under one's own power – 45%
Paralysis or being unable to run or scream – 42%
Taking exams – 31%
Missing a plane or train – 28%
Being naked in public – 15%

So don't worry. You are perfectly normal. As normal as the rest of the population, anyway. Dreams are dramatic and flashy – they want our attention. The fact that so many of us have similar types of dreams merely indicates that we have similar problems – and similar opportunities. There are just variations on a theme. And while the general type of dream may be shared by many, remember that within *your* particular dream will be individual, personal messages meant for you alone.

Let's take a look at some of the different types of dreams you may experience.

PHYSICAL INFLUENCE

"Last night I dreamed I ate a ten-pound marshmallow, and when I woke up the pillow was gone." Tommy Cooper.

There are times when dreams are influenced by your immediate physical environment. This is usually discovered quickly, and that part of the dream shown to be merely a reaction to an outside stimulus.

For example:

You hear a horrible ringing noise interrupting your dream banquet. As you stir, you find your alarm is announcing that it's time to get up for work.

You feel a sudden sharp pain in your ribs while cruising down the Nile. You awake to find your husband's elbow in your side.

There is a sudden chill in the air, although the sun is bright in your dream meadow. When you wake up, you find the covers have all been thrown off in your tossing and turning.

Don't look for deep hidden meanings for noise, pain, or chill in these dreams. It is obvious that your body has reacted to actual physical events which have filtered into your dreams. You might, however, get a bigger bed so that your husband can keep his elbow to himself!

PERSONAL GROWTH

"Human beings have an inalienable right to invent themselves." Germaine Greer.

Your dreams may start out being long, detailed, confusing, convoluted, and quite dramatic. You will often experience a series of three inter-related dreams, each with the same theme but using mixed symbology. As you work with your dreams over time, they often become increasingly simple, develop into bite-sized pieces, sometimes even just a brief image. You may one day see yourself at the top of a high hill, raising your arms in joy and wonder. This is the same hill you were struggling to climb in your dreams a few months back. Now here you are; you've made it!

As your knowledge and wisdom grow and your life skills mature, your dreams keep pace. They grow with you. You will notice a different tone, a grander scope, a change of scene. You may stop dreaming about crawling and feel yourself flying through the air. Your venue may move from high school to a university.

Feel encouraged. You have graduated. You are now being presented with advanced lessons, ever on the road to the truth and freedom. As you grasp each lesson and work on it, doing your homework faithfully, your dreams will again change.

Dream life is never dull.

SELF REVEALING

"The aim of life is self-development. To realize one's nature perfectly – that is what each of us is here for." Oscar Wilde.

As you grow, you will have many dreams that hold a mirror up to your inner and outer selves. These dreams are sometimes less than complimentary. The painful image may result in a "blocked" dream, which you just "cannot" remember; or just "cannot" decipher. It is often unpleasant (although very helpful) to face the less than perfect aspects of your own nature.

Self-knowledge covers a wide variety of topics. You are, after all, a greatly diverse individual, involved in many activities and relationships. You are of a nature that must coordinate a body, a mind, and a spirit.

Dreams address all of these parts of your self. They include wish fulfillment, suppressed desires, worries, problem solving, doubts, creative outlets, decision making, and much more.

Let's explore some examples of dreams exploring self and growth:

Catherine was having doubts about her ability to cope with life or make good decisions. She didn't feel worthy of the good things that were appearing in her life and inevitably took steps that put those good things in jeopardy. She began having dreams about being chased by a large, threatening man.

Fortunately, Catherine had a strong spiritual base, and decided to try to get rid of these dreams by using spiritual promises she felt were based in truth. In her next dream "chase scene" she turned around and faced the danger. She reports:

I kept saying "God loves you, God loves you" over and over again to the person chasing after me. This stopped the action. I woke, and immediately entered the dream in my log book. While working on interpreting this dream, I realized that the person chasing me was myself! I had to act on my belief that I too, with all my weaknesses, was loved by God, and that I was fully capable of taking on the challenge of turning my behavior around. The good things in life were, after all, being presented to me by God. Who was I to say I wasn't worthy? Things got a lot better after that, and there were no more ugly brutes chasing me in my dreams.

Joe was working on a book, one on positive thinking. He had recently published a technical book and was nervous about branching out into something new. He did feel this was an important topic, and had some ideas he thought were vital to get out there. As he pondered, he had this dream:

I was walking toward a place I had visited before in another dream. I took a different path this time, yet felt confident and self-assured. I was striding purposefully, recognized the way, and did not get lost (a fear of mine). The site waiting for me was a huge, architecturally grand cathedral or university, I wasn't sure which. It looked more like a cathedral, but I decided that it could be both.

I took this as confirmation that I was on the right path going to the right place, and proceeded full steam ahead. A major publisher bought my new manuscript. I received many thanks from readers who affirmed that my book had opened their eyes and made a real difference. I thanked the Universe for sending me that dream.

Mary was just starting college, on her way to a nursing career. She was taking multiple science classes, but had a mental block. She couldn't seem to wrap her mind around them, understand them, or study for the tests. She couldn't understand why this was so, as she had always had straight A's. A dream showed her the problem:

I saw a minister standing in a field flying a kite. A cross and a coin were imprinted on the kite. Suddenly a bolt of lightning hit the kite; the lightning traveled down the string and gave the minister a big jolt. He picked himself up off the ground with a look of amazement. He did a little jig. This reminded me of Franklin's discovery of electricity.

Mary then realized that she was having a mental conflict between her conservative religious upbringing, which denied much of the teachings of modern science, and what she was learning in college. The dream showed her that God and science can work together for the good of mankind. The cross on the kite symbolized the spiritual and the coin the material. The lightning, one of God's natural creations, brought to earth an idea that transformed the world.

Some of the most interesting dream experiences reveal the divided nature of man, and show the split-personality which lies beneath the surface of the average individual:

George, a ship's captain, was well educated and responsible. He took his life's work seriously. He knew, however, that aside from the actual physical and administrative side of his job, he loved the sea, the vast open spaces, the swell of the waves and the force of the wind. He wondered if this attraction to the raw and sometimes dangerous side of nature was normal. His dream gave him understanding:

I saw a tall, handsome man wearing a captain's uniform, similar to my own. Suddenly, his uniform ripped open, and I viewed an enormous gorilla peering out. The captain immediately knocked the gorilla on the head and restored his captain's uniform back to its proper place. I realized then that we all have some of our basic animal nature within us, but as long as we have control over those passions, we need not worry.

Sometimes we think we are doing the right thing, but need some help with variations on a theme:

Sue and her husband Doug had invited his mother to live with them. Doug's mom was up in years, couldn't climb stairs well, and her old home was in an isolated country area. Mom reluctantly agreed. However, she was a strong, independent woman, used to getting her way. The situation was stressful. Even Doug was losing patience with her. Sue's dream brought home the problem:

I heard much shouting and excitement. The windows of our house were open, and it was raining and storming outside. We rushed to close and lock them. Some terrible wild man was running through the town shooting and causing great trouble, and the police were chasing him.

Sue knew the wild man was her husband, whose temper was getting shorter and shorter. The situation as it stood was not going to get better. She did not want to reach the point where she didn't want her husband to come home, or wanted to shut him out. She told Doug about her dream, and suggested that they use some of the money his mom had received from the sale of her home to build a small separate cottage behind their main house. In this way they could all have their independence and privacy, yet Mom could still be monitored and kept safe. Doug immediately agreed.

As you can see, dreams of self revelation can warn, can suggest solutions, can encourage. Sometimes the interpretation will be immediately apparent, sometimes you have to dig deep. Keep on digging, you *will* find gold.

In case you are thinking you will need lots of help to mine all that gold, don't worry. Chapter 7 provides you with some heavy-duty tools.

MULTIPLE LAYERS

"If you were to ask me which of these interpretations is valid, I should have to respond that they all are. They all fall within the field of possible meanings created by the story itself." David C. Steinmetz.

You've written a dream in your log (more on this in the next chapter), mulled it over, gotten a handle on the symbology, and voila – come up with an interpretation. Later that day you suddenly perceive another meaning for the same dream. You see where the symbology could also apply to another facet of your life. Which is the correct interpretation, you wonder?

As you are eating dinner, another flash comes into your mind about this mysterious dream. It seems that it could have even another message for you. Boy, this is getting complicated, frustrating even.

Don't despair. This happens every once in a while. Dreams can have three levels of meaning, just as we have three levels of life experience – physical, mental, and spiritual. Sometimes the Universe feels especially helpful. We are then given a dream that shows us the overall picture of a life situation we are experiencing. This kind of dream takes a bit of work on your part. Think of an archeologist and the various levels he may have to dig through before he can flesh out the overall picture of a long-past civilization.

Tom's dream life provides a good example of this perplexing type of dream:

Tom was unhappy with life in general. He was gaining weight, saw wrinkles and gray hair in the mirror, was constantly arguing with his wife, and hadn't had a good laugh for months. He thought a vacation might do him a world of good, but couldn't get up the energy to make plans. It turns out what he really needed was a good old-fashioned dream.

In the midst of his angst, Tom entered this dream in his journal:

I entered a lush reception room; in the center of the room was a long, solid table. Waiters were rushing back and forth, filling the table with all sorts of food, drink, and decorative bouquets. As one would set down several platters of cold cuts, the table would tilt; another waiter would fly to the other end of the table and fill it with bowls of salad and trays of vegetables. The table would subsequently right itself.

Suddenly the roses in the center began to wilt, petals falling onto the elegant tablecloth. Coffee urns had been placed on each side of the vases. Heat from the urns was withering the beauty of the centerpiece. The waiters came to the rescue, moving the urns to either end of the table, and spraying the roses back to life with a crystal atomizer.

As I watched, I noticed a corner of the room where a young boy was holding a red balloon, watching "Leave It To Beaver" on a screen. Thoughts of "Beaver's" simple, uncomplicated days of yore brought a smile. I went over to watch the program with the child.

Tom mulled over his dream. He realized that his eating had become unbalanced (the tilting table). He had been getting lazy, stopping by Get-It-Now for a ham biscuit on the way to work, rather than having his usual poached eggs with wheat toast. Take his lunch? – no time for that. Easier just to send his secretary out for a Mega-Burger and Frenchie Fries at noon.

The stress at work and on his body had made him into a bit of a grouch. His testy replies (the hot coffee) to his wife, Rosa, had alienated her. Their relationship was wilting. He had to get out of this spiraling routine.

Simplicity. Perhaps that was part of the answer. He must let his energy soar (the red balloon), and get back to his true self. Once he got his priorities in order, his body would heal, his mind relax, and his spirit (the crystal atomizer) rise.

Tom got to work.

A three-layer dream doesn't have to be quite so complex. It can be short and sweet:

Joan was concerned about her marriage. Everything seemed fine, but her husband had been working a lot lately, and they hadn't been able to spend much time together. She missed this closeness. Then she experienced a strange dream:

"My dream is cloudy and surreal. I am writing a note to my husband, who is in the same room (communication, mental). He seems to know what I am putting onto paper, although I am not finished. I look up, and he extends his hand to me. We go into the bedroom, and I am happy (physical). Later I see two doves in our oak tree. They fly away together (spiritual)."

Joan awoke feeling that the stability and happiness of her relationship with her husband had been confirmed. They had good communication, although not always expressed (the first layer). They had a good physical relationship that was valued by both of them (second layer). And they had a spiritual relationship that was loving (two doves), strong (oak tree), and would last through death and beyond (they fly away together). This was the third layer. She had no further doubts.

WHAT, *AGAIN*?

"Any idea, plan, or purpose may be placed in the mind through repetition of thought." Napoleon Hill.

The Universe is quite persistent. It does not give up. If you don't work out an important message, you will get a second chance – and a third, and a fourth – until the light dawns.

Thus you may have similar dreams several nights in a row. You see the same theme expressed in different ways. The dream is increasingly dramatic or strange. This is done to get your attention. "Hey, you," your dream calls, "Listen up!"

Professor Karla Jones was in a dilemma. She taught physics at a top-level university but felt increasingly called to do research. Should she, or shouldn't she? She reports a series of dreams:

I was standing in a drab field. The grass was browning, flowers were faded, and weeds were beginning to spread. I looked across the road where there was another field. That field was well tended. Flowers were blooming, and the grass was green. I woke up quite perplexed.

The next night, Karla reports, she had a similar dream: I was in the same field as before, but this time the grass was definitely brown, the flowers were dying, and weeds were everywhere. The field across the way now had flowers in full bloom, tall trees, and birds flying overhead. What, Karla wondered, was going on?

On the third night, the scene was quite theatrical: My field was now quite dead. Black clouds floated overhead, there were no flowers, weeds had taken over, and brambles with large thorns had sprung up. The opposite field was radiant. Flowers of every color shone, birds sang, trees were burdened with fruit, and the sun was full. I was amazed, but still confused. Suddenly, a voice boomed out of the clouds (I guess the powers that be had given up on my thought processes). It clearly and forcefully told me, 'YOU ARE IN THE WRONG FIELD'." Well, Karla tells us, I finally got the point. I tendered my resignation and accepted the offer from ABC Research Lab. I am making great progress and am thankful for that thunderous message.

On the other hand, you may have only one dream, but that one dream is convoluted, involved, and goes on and on. It seems to be three or four separate scenarios, each one blending into the next. In reality, the same message is being expressed in various creative ways. It is sometimes hard to catch these lengthy texts on paper before images fade, but please try. You won't be sorry. Once you see the thread, all will be revealed.

If all else fails, you can always ask to have the dream repeated in a way that you will understand. More on that technique in Chapter 7.

I remember a series of dreams I had when I was working on my first book, *Secrets Your Bridge Friends Never Tell You*. The book is about the duplicate bridge world. I was looking for endorsements and also for an illustrator. I had endorsements from local experts, but approval from a national expert would be a big boost. My bridge partner and I occasionally consulted with such an expert by telephone when we had bridge dilemmas to resolve. Would he be willing? I also had researched, via the internet, for professional illustrators and found some that were reasonable but did not know the bridge world. My first choice was the illustrator for a national bridge publication, but surely he would charge a fortune. What to do?

Well, here comes my dream world, giving me encouraging advice:

Dream 1. I went into a restaurant and wanted a steak, but it cost $52.00. I looked over the menu and was going to get a hamburger, but when I saw the steak item on the menu again, it was only $12.00. I ordered the steak.

Dream 2. I saw a star in the sky; as I watched it admiringly, it floated down and sat next to me.

Dream 3. I was going to model a dress, but it didn't fit right. I was afraid to ask for another style but got my nerve up and asked the designer what he thought. I got the most fantastic dress in the show and knocked everyone out.

I concluded that I was being guided to go ahead and ask the 'stars' for what I wanted, that it wouldn't cost me what I was afraid it would, and that my readers would be quite impressed. The national expert said sure, he'd be glad to help me out. No charge. The illustrator I had my eye on, who was also a bridge player, quoted me a fee I couldn't afford. I sadly told him that my budget was pretty tight. He responded that this was a project he would really like to work on, and that we'd iron things out later. We became friends, his cartoons were super, and he said he'd be glad to take a small percentage of my royalties. Brave man. He might have ended up with nothing.

This experience reinforced in me the maxim that if you don't ask, the answer is *no*. I had to get bold and take a leap of faith. You really do meet some earthly angels in this life.

PROMISES

"God's promises are like the stars; the darker the night the brighter they shine." David Nicholas.

In her book, *When We Were Gods*, Carol Chapman tells of a dream that accurately depicted the man she was to marry! Carol was a struggling single mother. She had been dating a millionaire, who proposed. Unfortunately, while she admired and respected the man, she was not in love. She wanted to hold out for her soul mate, so could not bring herself to say "yes." Many thought she was crazy, but she stuck to her ideals.

She was then given a dream. The dream was about the actor "Godunov" who played the husband destined to marry the single mother in the movie "Witness." In Carol's dream, the actor lived on a hill in a house that he had designed, had a black Labrador retriever, and a dark-haired friend who had a dark-haired wife. There was also a satellite dish on site. The dream faded into another scene, where Carol saw a stage. In the spotlight center-stage stood a tall, husky man with reddish-blonde hair standing with his back to her. As if on a turntable, he slowly rotated until he was facing her. She liked how he looked. He smiled softly at her.

Upon waking, Carol thought this was confirming her decision not to marry the millionaire, and that she would find someone who would be "good enough" later on and who would take center stage in her life. (Many times plays on words will appear in dreams and the name Godunov sounded to her like "good enough".)

The next day, in the cafeteria of the building where she worked, she saw a man at the water fountain who looked familiar. As she walked by, she glanced at his face – he was the man in her dream! She found him wildly attractive. She couldn't bring herself to approach him, however, and after a few weeks she began to doubt that it meant anything at all. A whole year went by, and no one special appeared in her life. Eventually, however, she ran into John (the man at the water fountain) and decided maybe she needed to take action. He seemed rather shy. She told him she had dreamed about him. He thought it was one of the best lines he'd ever heard! She learned that he had been instrumental in the design of his home; that he had a black Lab; and yes, he had a dark-haired friend with a dark-haired wife. To top things off, his job was making simulators for satellites. It seemed the dream was indeed full of accurate details.

Perhaps the dream had been presented with such specific details so that Carol could not help but recognize this man, and eventually be assertive, since John was very quiet and shy. To make a long story short, after a year's courtship, they married. Carol had indeed found the man of her dreams.

Note that this dream initially took form because the dreamer made a difficult decision and stood by her ideals. Subsequently, the dreamer had to *take action*. It took her a while, but once she got up her nerve, her dream came true.

NIGHTMARES

"*Deep into that darkness peering, long I stood there, wondering, fearing, doubting, dreaming dreams no mortal ever dared to dream before.*" Edgar Allan Poe.

You wake in a cold sweat, your heart pounding. You are seized with uncontrollable panic. The dark room is threatening, intimidating. You reach toward the lamp. You try to regroup, but a feeling of dread and fear follows you, refuses to fade away. You have had a nightmare.

A nightmare is, very simply, a 'bad' dream. A nightmare has all the qualities of any other dream but focuses on your emotions. The emotions brought into play in the dream then follow you into your waking state. It takes several minutes to calm down and realize that what you experienced was, indeed, only a dream.

Although you initially don't want to relive such a dream, you must, most certainly, write that dream down. A nightmare addresses important issues, issues that you have either been avoiding, or are not aware of. It often represents a part of yourself you are uncomfortable with and from which you want to distance yourself, but which is like a dark shadow that chases you everywhere you go. The deeper part of your psyche wants to make sure you get to the bottom of your fears, anxieties, frustrations, guilt feelings – perhaps even aggressive behavior. It knows you might ignore a nice, sweet little dream filled with honey bees and flowers. So it gets dramatic – it wants your attention big time!

Once you sort through the imagery and understand the message, there is a shift. Rather than being terrified, you feel the comfort of knowing, the excitement and hope of being presented with a plan of action.

Of course there is always the possibility of a nightmare being a practical dream, a warning of impending danger. It is always good, after taking the above steps, to also offer up a prayer that such an event will not occur, and if it must, that it will be met in a positive way, with little harm, for the highest and best good of all concerned. You want to cover all bases.

Nightmares of Self-Discovery

A nightmare of 'self-discovery' commonly involves a person or animal chasing you, threatening you, or trying to kill you. You often lose your voice, cannot cry for help, or cannot run. There are other scenarios. You feel yourself falling into a deep hole or down a cliff. You may be lost or homeless, with no one to help you. You might try to use your cell phone to call for help but cannot manage to get the right number, or if you do, communication is fuzzy, or you are disconnected.

Several special techniques can help you translate your dream message. First, ask yourself what or who the danger represents. Is it part of yourself? Part of someone in your life? Are you perhaps threatening yourself?

Often, if you substitute images in a nightmare – change the monster to a bunny, or the cell phone to a pen – you get an 'aha' moment. You may realize that the boss you thought was a monster is really soft hearted and would listen, with his big ears, to your ideas. You might realize that you communicate better in writing, since you need time to think things out.

You might play a role – pretend you are the monster, or your voice box, or your cell phone. Then, as that image, speak to the you that is the dreamer. The monster may tell you he just wants you to tame him; your voice box may advise you to speak softly, that you're wearing him out; your cell phone might tell you that it's only a limited machine. This kind of work can be a lot of fun.

You can also imagine a different ending. This may lead you to realize what you really want, how to get it, what you need to do to address your particular issues. The imagination is a powerful tool. It can bring things from the inside out. Instead of falling off a cliff, imagine yourself taking off in flight, soaring above the clouds, feeling light and carefree. A lot more fun than landing spread eagle on the ground.

The Senoi, an ancient Malaysian tribe, believed that you must never run from a dream attacker but must instead fight back. Dreamers who try this soon find themselves winning easily. You may even befriend your attacker. If the attacker is some part of yourself that needs to be reconciled, this can be a good thing.

Let's look at some concrete examples of such dreams:

Marta dreamt of confronting a black wolf which was all-powerful; she felt it was evil, even though it never attacked her. It was as though it were stalking her. Marta had graduated magna cum laude from a prestigious school, taken the bar, and was working with a prominent law firm. She felt sure that becoming a junior partner was just around the corner. As she thought about the dream, she realized that the wolf, to her, symbolized a power that largely came from being part of a pack. The wolf itself was not evil. It was using its nature and instincts to survive and thrive. Marta realized that she associated herself with the wolf, as she was becoming a powerful woman within her group.

However, her early conditioning had programmed her to believe that being a powerful woman was evil. She was anxious, fearful that she would become socially unacceptable. Having a strong spirit, however, she was determined not to let her life stop because of outmoded ideas which she no longer considered valid. She sought help, became comfortable with herself, and was able to own her power and use it in a positive way.

Tim was a young boy, still small for his age. He was often afraid of boys who were bigger than he, and wondered if he were one of those 'scaredy cats' he had heard about. One night Tim had a nightmare about a monster that was chasing him, trying to tie him up. Tim evaded the monster, but then saw the monster going after his friend. Tim forgot his fear and rushed to save his friend. He yelled at the monster and ordered him to melt away. The monster looked shocked, but then did just that – melted onto the ground. When Tim had someone else to think about and to defend, he no longer felt helpless. He could get outside of himself, and become bigger than his fear.

When Tim woke up, he felt a calm joy, without knowing why. He told his mother the dream. Fortunately, she understood, and helped Tim understand. This dream revealed a great truth. Whenever we are drawn outside of ourselves, we find there is more to us than we realize. We come into contact with our highest and best self.

Help Me, I'm Dying

"What happens if I DIE in my dream?" you may ask. This is not an unusual concern. Believe me, you will not die in "real" life, as Bob and Brian discovered:

Bob found himself falling off a cliff from a great height. He continued to fall and hit the ground. Bob just got up, brushed himself off, and had no damage to his dream body at all. [He had been afraid of taking a long airplane flight.]

Brian dreamed that he was a spy and was killed by an enemy agent who had penetrated his cover. When he woke the next morning, however, he found he was still in one piece. Brian had been looking into some wrongdoing by a fellow employee, and was afraid of recriminations if his co-worker found out. Once he confirmed the information, he passed it on to higher ups, who then took charge. He was out of the picture, and suffered only temporary anxiety. He was also still above ground.

Personal Warnings

Sometimes a nightmare has another purpose. It wants to warn you of impending danger or disaster. If decoded, it can prevent automobile accidents, serious arguments, even save your life. It might save your marriage. It might keep your savings intact. These nightmares usually have more common, everyday images and distinctive, personal symbols:

Samantha had inherited a large sum from her grandmother. She was looking into investing it. She asked her new boyfriend, who was a broker, what he would recommend. He said he could take care of it for her.

That night Samantha saw a large snake slithering through the grass, coming toward her, mouth open, fangs ready. She started to run, but her feet were like lead. A large dark hole opened up in front of her. She looked to the side and saw an ax. She grabbed it and without hesitation, cut off the head of the snake. She looked into the hole and saw a blanket of dollar bills, which suddenly started to float upward toward her.

As Samantha analyzed her dream, she realized that the snake-in-the grass might be her new boyfriend, who was preparing to deposit her money into a black hole from which it would never return. She checked into his background and found that he had left his last position under a cloud of suspicion. She gave her new friend the old heave-ho and invested her funds safely with an established trustworthy firm.

Rick woke with a fright, having just dreamt that on the way to work a huge semi-truck had careened out of control and demolished his car. He saw himself being carried away in a screaming ambulance. He had ignored the red "Detour" sign posted just prior to the site of the accident, which would have taken him about a half-mile out of his way. He had been in a hurry and, seeing no road work, just kept on going. He had seen the truck coming, but was frozen in time.

The next day, Rick decided to take another route to work. He left early, and although he saw no detour sign, stuck with his intuitive hunch. Nothing dramatic happened, Rick worked away, and took the same route back home. As he settled down to watch the news, lo and behold, the screen produced an image of horrendous carnage left by a semi-truck which had crashed through a building front on the same road Rick had avoided that very morning. The reporter advised that no one had been hurt, as the intersection was surprisingly clear of traffic at a time when many were usually going to work. Rick resolved that he would never ignore his dreams, no matter what.

Recurring Nightmares

Quite often you have the same nightmare, or a variation of it, over and over again. "What is going on here?" you may ask. The nightmares are trying to get through to you about an issue that needs to be addressed. The dream is repeated because you are not dealing with that issue. "But," you cry, "I just don't understand the message!"

One thing you can do is ask for the dream to be presented in a way that you will understand it. The Universe is flexible and will be glad to oblige.

Another technique is to face the images in the nightmare and ask, "Why are you here? What do you want to tell me?" You avoid future nightmares by determining what it is in your life that makes you afraid, or feel helpless, or get angry. Then you work on yourself: perhaps ask for help, read a book, talk to a friend. It is the *unresolved* issues that cause recurrent nightmares.

Sandy had a recurring nightmare that was strange indeed. It was merely a vision of dark, swirling energy. She would wake with a strange dread, her heart pounding. Within a few days, her husband and son would have an angry shouting match with hurt feelings on both sides. The third time Sandy had the dream, she knew what was happening. She got frustrated – why was she having these dreams if she couldn't do anything about them? The light dawned. She could do *something*. She prayed that the angry interchange would not occur, or that if it must occur, that it would be softened and that things would be resolved harmoniously. Sure enough, a few days later the 'boys' got together again. This time, however, they kept their voices down, had a real discussion, and came to an understanding. Sandy's dream had a purpose; once she found out the reason, and took action, it all came together.

Pete was having issues at work. No matter what he did, he didn't seem to be able to get ahead. He was despondent and without realizing it, kept "shooting himself in the foot." He would miss a deadline; he would get too 'happy' at the company party; he would snap at his assistant. Of course, his dreams were bad too. An ugly monstrous figure would constantly seek him out, threaten him, come after him. Pete decided to confront this fiend. The next time the image appeared, he turned, looked directly at it, and repeated, "God loves you, God loves you, God loves you." It was the only thing that came to mind. When he awoke, he realized that the dream demon was indeed himself. His lack of self-esteem and fear of success were haunting him, keeping him back. If God loved him, well, then, he'd better love himself as well. He changed his attitude, cleaned up his act, and was promoted within six months.

With practice you can program yourself to turn and face your nightmare, to confront and overcome it. The images, no matter how fearful they seem to be, are usually part of yourself, or someone in your life. The monster you see has been conjured up to tell you something. The sooner you ferret out the truth, the sooner you will get rid of that nasty dream.

Night Terrors

With night terrors you sit up, often covered with a cold sweat; you're terrified but do not remember why. You're not fully awake. This type of occurrence is generally experienced by children. One explanation is that the child is experiencing intense stress on some level. Perhaps a grandparent has died or parents have divorced. If the experience persists, counseling can be helpful. Realizing what may be causing the terrors, a parent can often help the child understand and work through the trauma.

Another explanation, for those who believe in reincarnation, is that a past life experience still lives in the subconscious memory of the child, and is haunting him, so to speak. A hypnotherapist can often help. One 8-year-old who could not shake off his night terrors was taken to an exorcist as a last-ditch effort; he had no more problems.

The Science: Nightmares occur during REM (rapid eye movement) sleep. During this period, you are deeply lost in sleep, your daytime defenses are down, and you are tuned to receive valuable communications. This is the last stage of a sleep cycle and is most acute just before you awake. Dreams during REM are more easily remembered. We can deduce, then, that nightmares are important messages and are meant to be remembered (and written down, of course).

Night terrors, on the other hand, occur early in the sleep cycle, not during REM. You normally do not remember dreams from this period, which makes them almost impossible to write down or work with on a conscious level. They are "involuntary" dreams.

In conclusion, while not pleasant, nightmares bring you dramatic messages that can change your life in many astonishing ways, while night terrors may be deeply rooted in current or past-life traumas.

Do you ever wonder what Stephen King dreams about?

HELP ME, I'M FALLING!

"Sometimes it takes a good fall to really know where you stand." Hayley Williams.

Falling into a dark hole? Down a cliff? Flat on your face? These dreams are common and usually occur when you feel threatened by a situation, a person, or a challenge in your life.

John dreamt that he was jogging along a path. As he progressed, he felt compelled to go faster and faster, until he was running at breakneck speed. A large tree root had grown into the path in front of him, but he didn't notice. He fell spread-eagle upon the rough ground, bloodied and completely out of breath. In analyzing the dream, John recognized that he had become completely absorbed in his job, feeling the need to rush through things, get things done quickly. He realized he might overlook pitfalls on his personal path if this continued, and fall flat on his face, not to mention injure his health in the process. He knew he was being warned to slow down and create balance in his life.

Sue tells us, "I was walking briskly through a field. I realized I was approaching a drop-off that seemed steep. I just kept walking, straight off the cliff. As I fell, I realized I could never get back to the field." Sue was 30, and had been anxious to marry for the past two years. The eligible bachelor pool seemed limited. Kurt had just proposed, and she had accepted. She was very fond of Kurt, but wasn't sure he was The One. She was simply afraid to wait any longer. As she pondered her dream, she knew she could not take the plunge off that cliff. It wasn't right. She would have to wait until it *was* right, for her own sake and that of her prospective partner.

If you find yourself falling, falling, falling, ask yourself what's going on in your life that might make you take a spill. What decisions are you making? Who are you involved with? Do you need to make a change? Do you need to ask for help? What is the setting of your dream? The setting may indicate whether the message addresses your domestic, social, or career environment.

Of course, if you find the fall is exhilarating and exciting, you may be jumping for joy. One man was bouncing on a rooftop trampoline, and flew through the air, falling headlong onto a giant puffy heart-shaped pillow. You guessed it – he was falling in love.

Once you are satisfied that you get the message, take the action to avoid (or enjoy) those falls. You may soon have a dream that you are flying!

FLYING HIGH
"Once you have tasted flight, you will forever walk the earth with your eyes turned skyward, for there you have been, and there you will always long to return." Leonardo da Vinci.

Flying in dreams is usually accompanied by feelings of exhilaration and freedom. Some dreamers fly with arms stretched forward (Superman), some lift off the ground and float weightlessly. One dreamer flew with her hands on her car's steering wheel, even though she had left the rest of the car behind on the ground. (She evidently wanted to maintain control of her destination, even in flight.)

These dreams usually indicate that you are rising above the earth's 'gravity', above mere physical limitations, becoming your 'highest' and best self. You are making remarkable progress. At times, you may run into telephone wires that interrupt your smooth flight. After all, we are all somewhat limited by earthly energy and communication. We can't lose our physical side altogether. We can, however, integrate it with our spiritual and mental selves.

Is a celebrity your flight companion? What characteristics do you attribute to that person? Are you now in sync with those starry qualities, rising above the mundane after years of work? Flying with Warren Buffet? You are on your way to becoming a successful CEO. Steve Jobs is by your side? As a computer guru, you will be in popular demand. Accompanied by Mother Theresa? You are the ultimate caregiver. In the clouds with the Dalai Lama? Your meditation has reached a peak.

If you fly far above the earth, you've reached a high level of development. If you fly closer to the earth, you may have a ways to go to get to the heavens. Do you find yourself able to fly at will? That means it's always possible. Keep practicing.

HEALTH
"The part can never be well unless the whole is well." Plato.

Your subconscious is sensitive to the condition and needs of your body. Sometimes, out of the blue, you will have a dream that communicates this concern. A health dream has a different feel about it, and often uses unusual images and symbols to capture your attention.

Such dreams often guide you to better health, or warn of a physical condition that needs to be addressed. They may point out emotional issues which are affecting your health.

Sally's dream journal provides a good example:

I was at a banquet, and in the middle of a table laden with all types of food was a plate filled with a huge mound of mashed potatoes. No gravy, just a lot of mashed potatoes.

Sally continues. I went immediately to my Nutrition Almanac and looked up potatoes. I found that they contain a very high percentage of potassium. I added potatoes to my menu more often, and also started taking a potassium supplement. My energy level climbed and has been sustained ever since.

Kate dreamt about traveling in a small boat in a tunnel, similar to the "Tunnel of Love" you might find in a carnival:

All along the upper part of the tunnel, where the ceiling starts to curve, were various fruits and vegetables, stretching through to the end of the tunnel.

I realized I was symbolically traveling through a vein in my bloodstream, which apparently needed the nutrition of more fruits and vegetables in order to flow smoothly through my system. I loaded up on apples and grapes, beans and carrots, honeydew and watermelon. My body felt this love, and I was soon feeling stronger. My blood pressure went down, and my skin looked great. I could even watch my grandchildren for a whole afternoon.

Dreams sometimes use a house as a symbol for your body. Mildred found this to be true for her:

I entered my dream-house and found that all the windows were clouded over with dirt and dust. I had trouble seeing out of them and couldn't enjoy the view of the lake I so loved.

Mildred had no problem recognizing the windows as a symbol for her eyes. She immediately had them checked by her ophthalmologist who confirmed that Mildred was developing cataracts. Treatment was begun.

Dietary advice can be very specific. Kevin relays the following vignette of a dream:

I had been suffering with colds constantly all year. This was beginning to affect my overall health and my performance at work. I prayed for guidance and advice. That night I had a dream:

A hand appeared. It put 1 oz. of lemon juice into a glass and then added an ice cube. I started to take this concoction every day, and felt better within two weeks. I continue to drink this potion daily and have never had another cold.

George was working long, hard hours, driving forward in his ambition for a promotion. As his stamina started to wane, he received this warning:

I was looking over a white plain, with red roads leading to the center wherein there stood a large volcano, pulsing in the sun. Suddenly the volcano erupted, the roads split open, and the plain was filled with red-hot lava.

George could not help but connect the volcano with his heart, which was in danger from the pressure and tension he was inflicting on his body. He resolved to work fewer hours, delegate more responsibility, and look at things in a different light. A promotion would come when he was ready, and more importantly, still alive!

You may not always be sure if a dream is directing attention to your body, or if the symbolism has another meaning. If in doubt, assume the literal message and address your health issues. If indeed your dream means, for example, that you need to be more fruitful, or that you aren't seeing issues clearly, don't worry. You will get another dream, or series of dreams, which will clarify the message. The Universe doesn't give up after just one try.

DREAM SEX

"I recall the old story of the rather refined man who preferred sex dreams to visiting brothels because he met a much nicer type of girl that way." Vivian Mercier.

One benefit to having sex in your dreams is that you can be sure it's safe...

Actually, dreams about sexual encounters, or romantic involvement, are not always about sex! Sex is a way of being intimate, of sharing, of blending with another. It is creativity. It is love in physical form. Dreams about sex can reflect this symbology.

Creative Energy

You may be using your physical energy in a creative way. You may be excited about a project or a relationship. There may be a part of your personality that is awakening to being more open, more intimate, to having a closer relationship with others. Marta tells us about just such a dream:

She was in bed with her boss. They were lying close together, quite comfortably, but were just talking. She felt completely at ease. When she awoke, she was perplexed and a bit worried. She had no romantic feelings at all toward her boss, who was 30 years older and happily married. Then it hit her. She had submitted a business proposal recently, which had been accepted. She and her

---

boss were now working closely together on it and making good progress. They had gotten to know each other better and come to like and respect each other. They were 'in bed together', so to speak, for this project.

What's Your Partner Like?

The personality and characteristics of the person you're in bed with in your dream (or perhaps in real life as well) is telling. If the dream person is romantic and sweet, you may wish you could blend those qualities into your own persona, or you may wish your real-life lover had those qualities. Or it could be the opposite.

Lisa found herself dreaming of being in bed with her grammar school buddy, who was just a good friend. She realized that sex with her husband had become like being with a 'buddy'. She needed to graduate to high school. She went out and got some sexy lingerie and new perfume...

Obstacles

Obstacles often indicate difficulties you are having in a current, intimate relationship or with yourself. For example, Laura was happily married, but it seemed she was never alone with her husband. They had children coming and going, projects, work – a constant stream of concerns.

Laura dreamt that she and husband Rob were in a large room containing only a bed. They were in bed and getting ready to have sex. Suddenly one of the doors opened, and several people walked through the room and out the other door. The lovers once again turned to each other but were once more interrupted with doors opening and closing and people walking in and out. When Laura woke up, she realized how frustrated she was with the lack of privacy in her life. She talked to Rob, and they scheduled a romantic cruise. They did not invite anyone else. They also vowed to have a 'date night' once a week, so they wouldn't slide back into old habits.

An Unexpected Partner?

You may find yourself having sex with an unexpected partner.

John found himself in bed with his ex-wife. He woke up with a jolt, wondering what that was all about. He certainly did not feel intimate toward her anymore. Then he realized that his ex and his current 'steady' were very much alike in personality and habits. He'd better think about his choices and relationships in greater depth if he didn't want to repeat his mistakes.

In Bed with a Co-Worker/Friend

Having dream sex with a co-worker or friend? Once again, (of course), analyze your dream partner's qualities and characteristics.

Julia found herself in bed with Tim, a co-worker who was friendly and reliable; a truly kind, well-balanced guy. The sex was rich, warm, and sexy. She was surprised, as she wasn't attracted to Tim in real life. She then realized that none of her boyfriends were like Tim; her picks were usually exotic and unusual. She thought she'd like to feel comfortable with a boyfriend for a change. She decided to try looking for more than a flashy exterior and see what happened.

A Famous Person Appears

Your dream finds you in bed with a celebrity! Just as with non-celebrities, you must ask what this person represents to you. What personality traits are associated with this star? Do you secretly want to be like him/her? Is there someone now in your life who reminds you of this famous person? How did you feel in this dream?

Patti found herself in bed with Johnny Depp. While her dream sex with Depp was exciting and romantic, Patti found that Johnny was always joking around and would never get serious. It reminded her of her husband. They really must have a talk.

Paul dreamt of Angelina Jolie. She was beautiful and exotic, but never quite ready to commit. He realized that his current girlfriend struck him exactly that way. Should he enjoy the relationship while it lasted, or was that self-destructive? He'd have to decide.

A Former Lover Reappears
Has a former lover popped up in your dream bed? An analysis of the dream lover may shed light on your romantic choices, perhaps indicate a repetitive pattern in your love life. Do you always want the flashy, sexy look? How do these choices turn out? Is it important to stroke your ego by being seen with a 'looker'? Does the thought of a deeper, mutually beneficial relationship scare you?

Family Members
Do family members invade your sex dreams?

Shirley was having sex with her boyfriend, when he suddenly turned into her father. She was stressed and disturbed. Analyzing her dream, Shirley knew she had always recognized the domineering and controlling part of her father but had missed it, or dismissed it, in her boyfriend. She was now able to see this aspect clearly, and knew she must break off the relationship and move on.

Your Lover Leaves You – Or Vice Versa

Your lover runs off with someone else? How dare he! This dream may expose an affair, one that you have probably suspected. Typically, though, the dream deals with issues in a relationship:

In Cindy's dream, she was happily clinging to her boyfriend Mark's arm, when he suddenly shook her off and ran out the door of the pub. Cindy was devastated and embarrassed. She was sure he was chasing after a cute blonde who had been sitting next to them. On waking, Cindy realized she was too dependent on her lover, that her self-esteem was tied to him, making her overly jealous and suspicious. She knew this weakness would eventually alienate Mark. She sought professional help.

Jerry dreamt that his new girlfriend took off with another guy. Jerry realized he was insecure, but also recognized that his girlfriend was not ready to make a commitment. In waking life Jerry exuded confidence, but in his dreams he had to face his fears – and reality. If he wanted a more lasting relationship, he'd have to be patient and not pressure Sue for any immediate decision about an exclusive relationship.

Carl's dream girlfriend walked off with a sexy, aggressive player. Carl realized that, without any basis, he was worried he couldn't satisfy his highly sexual partner. He had a chronic insecurity with her, and his dream was pointing this out. If he didn't turn things around, he might lose her in real life. He decided to talk to a counselor about boosting his self-esteem.

Sometimes *you* do the leaving:

Brandon's dream found him leaving his lovely brunette girlfriend for a sexy blonde. His girlfriend used to be what Brandon thought of as a sexy blonde type, but she now wanted a deeper relationship, and he wasn't ready. He'd have to decide what to do.

Unwanted Sex

Sexual coercion in a dream can be traumatizing. This kind of dream may reflect that you are feeling cornered, held down, or violated. This may be occurring at work, within a relationship, or in your family environment. The way the dream ends usually indicates how you are coping with the situation.

Gina dreamt that her boss had called her into his office, thrown her on the couch, and attacked her. Gina was in a panic, but suddenly punched him in the face, threw him off, and ran out of the door. When Gina awoke, she realized that she constantly felt put-down by her boss, who criticized her every move, and was holding her back from a promotion. She needed to either fight back, or leave the job entirely. She thought she might also take a karate class, just in case.

However, the dream can also be a signal of prior (or current) sexual abuse. Take these dreams seriously and seek help.

In Summary

Sex dreams can be using sexual symbology to open your eyes, give a heads up, make a commentary, or encourage, just as any other type of dream does. It may also be a reflection of your desires, your love life, or your physical attraction to another. As always, it's up to you to interpret your very own very personal dreams.

MIRRORED DREAMS

"There are more things in heaven and earth, Horatio, than are dreamt of in your philosophy." William Shakespeare.

You are talking to your sister about a disturbing dream you had the night before. Halfway through she interrupts, "Wait, wait a minute. I know this dream." She then proceeds to tell you what happens, blow by blow. You are astounded. How can this be? You both had the same dream on the same night!

These "mirror" or concurrent dreams happen more frequently than you might think. There is usually a close connection between the dreamers, as well as a mutual concern or interest. An unconscious ESP exists between the dreamers, which the Universe ties into. "Well," the Universal Forces plot, "Let's get two birds with one stone."

You may ignore your own dream, especially if it's advice you don't want to hear, but when you learn that your dearest friend has had the same dream, it's a double whammy that is hard to push aside.

Sometimes the two dreamers may not communicate for some time and only learn later that they each had the same message. By that time, it may be too late for the desired result. The opportunity for action may have passed. So call your daughter (friend/neighbor/ co-worker) the very next day if you have a strong dream about her. She will be flattered that you have dreamt about her, and you can relay the dream as though it were an interesting story. She will know you have had her on your mind. You need not make a big deal about it. She will get a message if there is one, and if the message was for you alone, oh well, you've had a fun conversation with your daughter (friend/ neighbor/co-worker). Every once in a while, however, you might even hear that she has had a similar dream. Your input will reinforce the importance of the event, and you'll be glad you called right away.

Let's eavesdrop on Martha and her best friend, Chelsea:

Martha is concerned about the latest guy her friend Chelsea has taken up with. He is good looking and charming, but there is something about him that just doesn't seem to ring true. Martha is afraid he may be more interested in Chelsea's inheritance than in Chelsea herself.

One night Martha has a strange dream. She sees Chelsea sporting about town with a huge Lion. They are having a grand time. When they arrive back at Chelsea's place, however, the Lion goes into the back yard, takes out a match, and proceeds to burn all the wood Chelsea has had cut for her fireplace.

Martha immediately enters the dream in her dream log, so she won't forget one tiny bit of it. She knows this is important. It may even be life altering for her friend. She dials Chelsea immediately.

As Martha starts to exclaim about her dream, Chelsea excitedly interrupts. "Let me tell mine first," she says. "This is a doozy." As Chelsea begins to relay her story, Martha practically falls on the floor. Chelsea's dream mirrors her own! Now she knows this dream was not just due to that piece of key lime pie she had before bed.

The two friends eventually unravel this mystery. The Lion symbolized Chelsea's boyfriend, who liked to be "King of the forest". A play on words also seemed to fit. Substitute "lying" for "lion," and more of the story unfolds. In the backyard of the Lion's mind was that pile of logs – the money saved up for the winter of Chelsea's life. He proceeds to "burn it up" without a thought, using a single match.

Chelsea admits she has had some reservations, some little clues here and there. She promises to investigate. She finds that most of the Lion's stories and background have been false. She gives him the boot without a backward glance. She is very grateful for this shared dream coming to her attention in such a spectacular way. She might have otherwise written it off as just another incomprehensible silly nighttime drama.

Admittedly this type of dream is relatively rare, but when in doubt, share. If nothing else, your confidant will enjoy a good story.

LUCID DREAMING

"Though no one can go back and make a brand new start, anyone can start from now and make a brand new ending." Author Unknown.

Are you suddenly aware you are dreaming? Are images crystal clear and colors vivid? Does memory of the dream linger long after you awaken? If your answers are yes, you have had a lucid dream. According to dream researchers, this type of dream is experienced by only 5-10% of the population, and even within that small group, such dreams are infrequent.

How does a dream become lucid? You are dreaming along, perfectly happy with the unfolding scenario, when suddenly you think, "How odd things are, this can't really be happening – *I must be dreaming!*" Or, you may recognize the dream as one you've had before and thus know what's going to happen next. This jogs your mind to realize that you are dreaming. You may be so frightened by a nightmare that you try to wake up, which again leads to the realization that it's all a dream. Flying dreams can also lead to lucidity, because of the intense pleasure and freedom you feel.

To stay lucid you need to maintain a degree of detachment. Once you forget you are dreaming, you are back in regular dream mode.

So what is so great about lucid dreaming? As long as you remain conscious, you can ask questions of your dream companions, you can make changes in the dream, you can experiment. In other words, you can attempt to interpret the dream, or use the information in the dream right on the spot. You can be both scriptwriter and director of your dream, then observe the benefits or consequences of any chain of events you set into motion. You can be creative in your approach to problems and innovative in looking for solutions, without worrying about what anyone else is going to think or how they will be affected.

Lucid dreaming allows artists to see what a new painting or sculpture might look like, architects to check out new designs, or scientists to play out experiments. A screenwriter can see how the movie will look, or a musician can listen to a new piece. Ideas can be played out with vivid imagery and few boundaries. The dream state, lucid or not, allows much greater freedom in creativity than the waking state. It allows your inner self to be brought into consciousness.

Facing and overcoming a monster in a lucid dream is another possibility. Ask the menacing 'thing' or person, "What are you here for?" or "Who or what are you?" This usually brings about a response and often a transformation of the image into something much more friendly. The images, after all, come from within yourself and are therefore representative of you or someone in your life.

You do not, however, have to control your lucid dream to benefit from it. In fact, it is *very rare* to be able to do so. Merely being a conscious observer in a dream allows you to learn more about yourself and ask yourself important questions.

Can you train yourself to have lucid dreams? It is possible. As with everything else, you must be motivated, not just curious. You must intend to be lucid, to remember, and to use what you learn. Lucid dreams should not be taken lightly. They can provide incredible insight and free your creativity and imagination.

Follow the same techniques you use to help you remember your every-night dreams. Program yourself, repeating your mantra ("I will be lucid in my dreams and will remember my dreams" is a suggestion) before bedtime. Don't become discouraged. If you cultivate one lucid dream a month you will be doing well. Then, of course, write your dream down and work with it. If you were lucid in only part of the dream, highlight that section in your Dream Journal (which you keep by your bedside, of course, along with a pen).

Most lucid dreamers find reading in a dream impossible. Even if you are able to read, for example, a street sign, it may still be impossible to remember the name of the street upon waking. If this is your experience, it's perfectly normal. If you see a street sign in your dream and know it's important, you can try to program yourself to wake up immediately, while repeating the name of the street. It is not likely it will work, but it's worth a try. It may be best, when you see the street sign, to focus on what it may mean, and let it soak into your consciousness. This way, whether you remember the name or not when you awake, you will get the benefit of the dream's direction. It will be stored away for future use.

Tim reports having a lucid dream that was a bit frustrating. He tells us that he was walking along a city sidewalk and was about to step off the curb. He then realized that he was dreaming, and had dreamt this same dream multiple times. Each time he stepped off the curb, he would be transported to another location.

He decided not to step off the curb this time. To his dismay, he was transported to the other location anyway! He had not been able to control the dream, but being lucid did bring the dream to his attention in a dramatic way. He wrote it down, worked with it, and discovered that he had a habit of stepping off the safe walkway in life, and into a world that was not in his best interests. He curbed his 'walks on the wild side' and transferred his need for excitement to the local community theater, where he became quite a star.

Caitlin dreamt, again in a repeating dream, that she was in an upstairs apartment with a group of people at a small party. She noticed a young child in a closet that had no door. The child's eyes seemed to follow her. She recognized the dream and decided to ask the child what she wanted to tell her. The child would not answer. Caitlin knew then that the child was part of herself that she was keeping hidden away, and that she would have to find out how to free the child on her own. Fortunately, there was no door on the closet. It didn't take Caitlin long to learn how to have fun and enjoy life outside of her stressful job.

Fran, an ambitious businesswoman, found herself being chased by a big ugly man, through streets, parks, and office parking lots. Suddenly it hit her, "This is a dream; I'm going to turn right around and confront this man." She asked him who he was, and what he wanted. He looked surprised. He readily replied, "I'm your feminine self – you've been running from me for ages. I'm not really ugly. Let's be friends." She was astonished. She realized the truth of his reply, however. She was hiding a very real part of herself because she thought it would hinder her success. Her tough-guy masculine approach wasn't the real her. Perhaps a more tactful, charming persona would be welcomed. She decided to stop role-playing and found that she was received enthusiastically. Her very real talents and very real self were more than enough for success.

FALSE AWAKENINGS

"If you want to make your dreams come true, the first thing you have to do is wake up." J.M. Power.

With a false awakening, you feel you have awakened, when in reality you are still dreaming. Often you truly awaken moments later, surprised that it wasn't real the 'first' time.

A false awakening may be filled with a kind of dread. For example, the dreamer may hear someone hammering on the door to the bedroom in a horribly threatening manner, as if a giant stood outside, about to burst in. Some report that when 'waking' in this condition, the whole room seems to be under tension. There is an atmosphere like an electric storm.

Other false awakenings are more gentle. The dreamer may test to see if he is awake, mistakenly concluding 'yes'.

False awakenings sometimes lead to lucidity (see "Lucid Dreams") if the dreamer isn't fooled. He then continues to dream, fully aware that he *is* dreaming.

There is no big message with a false awakening. It happens when the dreamer is ready to wake up but has trouble exiting the dream world. You soon wake up for real and get on with your morning coffee and newspaper. Not to worry.

WAKING DREAMS

"Those who dream by day are cognizant of many things which escape those who dream only by night." Edgar Allan Poe.

The Universe is not limited in its communication skills. It often tries to give you messages and helpful hints while you're awake!

Stay alert and aware. A series of similar events or circumstances will manifest as you go about your daily life. These will be pertinent clues to a current situation or puzzle you are facing.

For example, at my office I very rarely had to access the bottom filing cabinet. For two weeks straight, everything I needed was suddenly in that bottom cabinet. I had to bend down and reach for those files. I should have gotten the drift after the first week, but sometimes I'm a bit thick. Finally I said, "Hey self, what's going on?" The light dawned. I was being advised to bend a little. I needed to be humble and flexible in order to get to the truth of a matter, to get the information I needed to get to the "bottom" of things. I am a Taurus and a first born. Need I say more? (For those of you not familiar with these subjects, Taurus's are notoriously stubborn and first borns can be independent know-it-alls.)

That night I made a stew and thought I had done a pretty good job. After dinner, my husband said to me, "Let me make it next time, Cathy, OK?" I walked off in a huff, thinking he was commenting in a negative way about the quality of my cooking.

The next day, when my husband came home from work, I went into the bedroom while he was changing. I asked him about the stew and just what was wrong with it? He looked at me with surprise. He said there was nothing wrong with it, but that it was one of the dishes he enjoys cooking, and since he didn't cook that often, he'd rather that I save the stew for him to dabble with on his day off. I was stunned. After 34 years of marriage, we still had these miscommunications. Keeping my waking dream in mind, I decided to spend a few such minutes with my husband when he came home from work and talk over the day, including anything that might be bothering either one of us. We ended up getting some good insights and understanding each other's mindsets like never before. I had 'gotten to the bottom' of another challenge.

Sometimes we're being given a little gift. I wanted a new pair of slacks that had to be just so. I'd looked everywhere, no luck. I then received two fliers within a short time, touting sales by a local department store. I resolutely threw them away. Finally, I received a third flier, with a bigger and better-than-ever sale. Finally, the light dawned. Didn't the universe know I wanted those slacks? Weren't they trying to help me out? I took that flier, with its ever-so-helpful coupon, and went right to that sale. Bingo. I got my slacks.

On occasion, when I'm riding down the main highway in the county, every traffic light stays green. Wow! On another day, it happens that each time I approach an intersection the light turns yellow. Of course, there are also those days when I hit a bright red light every time. I mean each and every time. By the end of each of these trips, I know I'm being given a hint. That project is a GO; or, use CAUTION, there may be some snags here; or, STOP, do not even consider that action, you silly woman. I pay attention, believe me.

What convinced me? A friend begged me to loan him a large sum of money. He was desperate, but assured me he had a windfall coming within six months and would pay me back with 20% interest. This was tempting. I was advised by several confidants that the whole thing just didn't sound right. In addition, for three days I hit nothing but red lights. Did I listen? I wish I could say I did. I loaned him the money, my eyes glittering at the thought of that 20%. Of course, the six months stretched out to nine, and then twelve, and by that time I knew. I lost my money, never mind the interest, and had only myself to blame. I now pay close attention to those red lights. And to my real friends.

There are some events that are so big, often so traumatic, that you know they are special messages. They may show you part of your life's path, assure you that you have a contribution to make, perhaps let you know you're not alone. Claudia tells us:

When I was three years old some older kids, thinking it was funny, pushed me into a putrid lily pond that was almost seven feet deep. They all ran off laughing. I had no swimming skills but miraculously managed to get out. Covered in "muck" and stinking with seaweed, I returned home to a shocked mom. I told Mom that when I had looked up from the bottom of the pit, a hand had reached down into the water and pulled me out!

Although she tried to discover who he was, Mom never found the "good Samaritan." The result of that episode, however, was that our neighbors then wired, fenced, or drained all their hazardous water holes.

This incident imprinted in my very cells the promise that no matter what happened, or who did what to me, I had a guardian angel ready, able and willing to pull me out of trouble. It also gave me the knowledge that my ills and trials would be of benefit to others, perhaps even be a conduit to save lives.

The Confirmation:

Claudia did go on to have some fairly serious disappointments and trials. However, she remembered her promise, always stayed upbeat, and took action to turn her situation around.

Claudia loved children, but was never able to have any of her own. She joined the "Big Brother-Big Sister" program, and vowed to look for just the right 'little sister'. Her wait was rewarded, and she and Julia fell in love with each other. Julia became like the daughter Claudia had always wanted. She made sure Julia got a college education. Julia announced her engagement. Claudia suddenly decided to buy a new car, although her old one was only two years old. Sure enough, she presented Julia with her 'old' Cadillac for a wedding present. What path would Julia have followed had Claudia had children, and not gone looking for a little sister? No one knows. But we do know Julia was given some great opportunities through Claudia's initial heartbreak.

Claudia also is alive today when all odds were against it, more than once. In her own words, "I suffered the most egregious conduct by doctors, only to marvel afterward that I'd survived their life-threatening misdiagnoses, negligent conduct, and/or reckless disregard for the human condition. These were *multiple* experiences. It still baffles me that I'm here."

Yet when such incidences occurred, Claudia (with the help of her angel) not only pulled herself out of them, but went on to help others – sometimes large groups – to avoid such pitfalls. She was a journalist and was not afraid to speak up.

It appears that Claudia's early brush with death was indeed a waking dream, outlining to her the path her life would take. It gave her confidence, gave her life meaning, and steeled her resolve to survive and take action when life dealt her a blow.

Nature Provides a Waking Dream:

My husband grew the best tomatoes in the County. They were big and bright and tasted like a bit of heaven. We went without tomatoes all winter. The store-bought were like cardboard after having Russ's home grown.

I would watch Russ lovingly prepare the soil each spring, fertilizing it with careful measures of just the right stuff. He would choose just the right spot, where the sun could maximize its contribution to his babies. He would choose just the right seedling plants, healthy and strong. Once in place, he would water them faithfully, and later on, weed them faithfully. He would pick any nasty-looking bugs off the plants by hand. He didn't mind if the critters got a few; he knew there would still be plenty for us.

When the crop came in, we would promptly take the closest tomato and eat it right there in the field, letting the juice drip on the ground, and often on ourselves. I would thank my husband, and give an upward glance toward the sky, thanking the Universe and nature as well.

Isn't this a perfect picture of how to produce good results for our lives? We need to provide ourselves and our families with the best of environments. We need to plan for our best growth, nurturing ourselves with good thoughts, good food. We need to weed out anything that would harm our fulfillment and beauty. Nature provides a continuous waking dream.

In fact, nature's voice belongs in the "three-layer dream" category, giving comment on the three components of our daily lives: body, mind and spirit.

VISITATIONS
"When angels visit us, we do not hear the rustle of wings, nor feel the feathery touch of the breast of a dove; but we know their presence by the love they create in our hearts." Unknown

A loved one who has passed on has something to tell you or something to ask you. Their energy, their love, is still connected to you via spirit. They come to you while you too are in spirit, in your dream world.

A true visitation differs in subtle ways from a dream that is just 'about' a departed loved one. The dream feels realer than real: colors are brighter, light a little more refined, conversations more fluent. You remember specific details. You know somehow that you've had a real interchange, a real conversation with your deceased mother, husband, sister, friend.

When you wake up from the dream, you are positive that you have experienced something real. You had more than just a dream. As you write in your journal, the level of your memory is of a high quality. You easily recall textures, smells, the tilt of a head, a quirky smile.

The dream doesn't evaporate from your mind during the course of the day. Something remains with you, follows you. This is a signal that something special has happened, that you have connected. You have been comforted, advised, consulted, perhaps warned. What a wonderful world, this world of dreams.

The Spirit Needs Reassurance
My grandfather died suddenly of cancer when he was 60. We were stricken and in shock. He was beloved by all, a gentle, kind man, with a zest for life clear in his light blue eyes. He stayed obviously in love with my grandmother through 25 years of marriage. My favorite image of the two of them is at the kitchen table, having finished their Sunday waffles, holding hands.

Grandpa was a minister early in life, but subsequently divorced and left the church. He met my grandmother, who had also been divorced, and they were at each other's beck and call from then on. It was a "love at first sight" true story. The day after he died, he came to me in a dream:

Grandpa was distraught and began to tell me of his failings, real or imagined, whether in this life or another. Part of this, I'm sure, was because he felt he had betrayed his faith, with the divorce and remarriage. His voice expressed doubt as to whether he was worthy of meeting God.

I was aghast, and was intense in relaying my belief that any and all that was negative in his past was just that, in the past. I was passionate in my plea to remember all the good he had done, the love he had spread, the solidity, the comfort, the normalcy he had restored to our otherwise often dysfunctional family. He had given love and had been loved. What more could matter?

There was no reply, but his image faded. I knew this had been a real spiritual communication with Grandpa's spirit. I heard from him no more. I took that as a good sign. I felt he had been reassured and thus was able to go through the light to the other side without fear.

Helping a Loved One Cross Over

Gerald's father died in a coma, without ever knowing what had happened. A week after his father's death, Gerald had a dream:

His father was sitting at a table with his back toward Gerald, trying to fit the pieces of a jigsaw puzzle together. The father was unaware of his son's presence and was trying to figure out what had happened.

Gerald had heard about prayers for those who have passed. He decided to contact his spiritual adviser. His friend advised him that a soul sometimes does not realize that the body is no longer available; the soul can remain trapped in the "inter-between" for a long time. Ultimately the soul realizes what is going on and continues its journey to God and the life of spirit. This period of involvement in the "inter-between" can be shortened by the prayers of those still living in the earth plane, such as family and friends. Gerald requested help from a prayer group and sent prayers up himself. Soon he no longer dreamt about his father, which he took as good news. He felt his father had been released.

Helping Those Left Behind

Loved ones can still send you love and support, even when they're no longer on this earth. They sometimes visit you in your dreams, pray for you, arrange for serendipitous treats. I will share my own story:

Mom has been gone a while now. I used to dream about her frequently. I know she's happy and carefree, her spirit blending with the Universal forces of love that she shared so unselfishly. My recent dream experience shows me that she's still sharing:

I awake this morning with Mom's image still in my mind. She came to visit last night, along with my daughter Suzanne (who is still on this side of earth). We were sitting around the living room, comfortable and companionable. Mom promises me, "I'll help you through the tunnel, Cathy, don't worry." Suzanne gives me her little quirky smile, and says, "I'd help you too, Mom, but you know I hate that tunnel." We all laugh.

As I write it all down, I feel safe and secure. I am hoping, of course, that it won't be any time soon that Mom will help me through the tunnel! But I know that when the time comes, she'll be there. It is a comfort. I am reassured, too, knowing that there is no sense of time in spirit, so her promise is unlimited in scope. I always could count on Mom.

In case you're not familiar with "the tunnel," it is a term used for when we cross over from this life to the next, following a tunnel of bright light that leads us forward.

Here is another dream where a mom decided to step in from beyond the grave. It seems mothers never give up:

I dreamt of my deceased mother, Daniel tells us. She appeared to me and said "I am alive. Something is wrong with your sister's leg. She ought to see a doctor about it." I described the dream to my sister, and urged her to take it to heart. She told me her legs had been swelling, were a bit red, and felt warm, but she thought this was because she had been doing more walking lately. She reluctantly agreed to go to the doctor, who found that she had a blood clot which could have eventually caused a stroke. Treatment quickly followed and Sis was fine. We don't know how she did it, but we both raised our eyes, and said "Thank you, Mom."

Communications from Unknown Spirits

A spirit whose body has passed from the earth (a more melodramatic term is "ghost") may appear in dreams from time to time. A spirit uses the energy of mind or soul that is capable of telepathically sending detailed information. A dream communication is less frightful to humans than the alternate method of presenting itself in a ghostly form.

The Ghost of Lois. A young boy and his family moved into a large country home in Georgia. Soon afterward, Tim found a delightful new friend inhabiting his dream world. Her name was Lois, and she confided that this was really her house. She had grown up there, married there, and lived in the house all her life. Her father had built the house in 1917. She loved her home, and didn't see the need to go anywhere else. Tim noticed that she could change her age at will. For each chosen age, she would share her thoughts and activities as experienced at that age. For Tim, it was like going to the movies. As Tim got older, the dreams were less frequent, and Lois eventually faded away. Tim always thought he felt a certain presence in the house, but didn't connect it with his dreams until years later. He researched the town's archives and found that the first owners of the house did indeed have a daughter named Lois.

Release. It is beneficial to try to release a spirit from its clinging to the earth. The spirit must move on into the world of spirit to continue its journey and learn more about its purpose. You can pray for the spirit and ask that it be freed from its fear or reluctance to move on. There are also people who will come to your home who are trained to help a spirit move on.

Perhaps Oda Mae said it best: "He's stuck, that's what it is. He's in between worlds. You know it happens sometimes that the spirit gets yanked out so fast that the essence still feels it has work to do here." *Ghost*, the movie.

WHAT'S IN MY FUTURE?
"The future is called "perhaps," which is the only possible thing to call the future. And the only important thing is not to allow that to scare you." Tennessee Williams, *Orpheus Descending*, 1957.

Dreams foretelling future events happen more than we can know. They are often disguised, giving us no idea that this particular dream is sending a message of what is to come.

Dreams of prediction can forecast events to come within days, weeks, months, sometimes years. You may not even recognize them as precognitive dreams. If you feel a dream may be advising or preparing or warning you about the future, it is best to take the dream literally, even if you are not sure. At the same time, you can work on interpreting the dream from an everyday standpoint as well.

One reason you have precognitive dreams is to prevent danger. However, becoming obsessed with a warning can actually produce negative results. You may become so paranoid about avoiding an accident that you put yourself into other dangers, or even into the danger you hoped to avoid. For example, a dream warns you about bumping into a ladder, which causes you to fall onto the concrete, which gives you a concussion. You start looking everywhere around you for the miscreant ladder, everywhere but straight ahead... Of course, you miss seeing the ladder, and bango! The moral: always engage common sense.

The purpose of some futuristic dreams seems to be to prepare you so that you won't be taken too much aback when the time comes. Some dreams may let you in on a "secret", such as an unexpected windfall. Others may warn of an upcoming event that may be charged with negative energy and that will be upsetting to household or workplace.

There are times when intuition and energies are so strong that they fill the common consciousness of a neighborhood, state, or nation. This was experienced prior to 911 when multiple dreamers saw planes, devastation, and confusion in nightmares whose images closely mirrored the actual event which followed.

Let's look at some examples:

<u>Advance Notice</u>
I dreamt that I was on the lawn at my grandmother's house, looking at her front porch. I noticed that her rocking chair was gently swaying back and forth, although no one was in it. I noticed a hazy glow surrounding the chair. The scene felt calm and tranquil. A few weeks later, my grandmother passed away, and while I grieved, I was not surprised. I thought back on my

dream, and realized it was giving me advance notice of grandma's passing, reassuring me she would be all right and at peace.

Secret Revealed

My husband, Russ, and I were visiting my Dad in Reno, staying at a hotel overlooking the mountains. The night we arrived, I dreamt I was rummaging through the freezer compartment of our refrigerator at home. I turned toward Russ and said, "There's no more rocky road (ice cream)." I was in the middle of writing a book, and quickly surmised that I would have a smooth road finishing it up (wishful thinking). I was also concerned about a credit card debt that loomed on the horizon, especially since Russ was set to retire in a few months, but that issue didn't come to my mind at the time.

I had a date with Dad at his favorite casino the next morning. Russ said his hellos, left us to visit, and went on to take his chances at poker. Dad got us coffee, and we sat down to chat. He announced that he was distributing his estate to his children early, while they were of an age to enjoy it and when it could make a difference. He also wanted to be able to see them enjoy it and vicariously participate in their adventures. I was overwhelmed. It was totally unexpected – but wait. That rocky road ice cream. This was what it was all about. The rocky road of debt was now to be eliminated. My little dream had foretold this very moment, and so cleverly. Had the event not followed immediately, I might have missed the delight of the connection entirely. Those sneaky dreams!

Warnings

Sarah, age 17, relays a dream with a very definite, concrete warning:

In my dream I was at a house that I didn't recognize, but I seemed comfortable. I was watching TV. A guy I seemed to know came in (when I woke up and thought back about my dream I realized I didn't really know him in waking life). He asked me if I wanted to go get food. He seemed drunk. However, I said yes and we walked outside to his car. We stopped right in front of his car for a second for no apparent reason. Then we got in and started to drive away. He was driving. When we got onto the main road, he ran a red light and we crashed into another car. That was the end of the dream.

Two months later I was in a house that mirrored the one in my dream. It was my dad's new house. The guy from my dream was his roommate. I had met him during the two months following my dream. He came home drunk one night and I realized, the minute he walked in the door that things were unfolding just like in my dream from two months ago. We walked out to his car, and when we stopped in front of his car, I told him about my dream; I took the keys and drove. I stopped at a red light. It was the red light he had run in the dream. The same car he had hit in my dream drove past us. I had a really weird feeling when I saw the car.

In the above dream the future event occurred in a relatively short period of time. However, some dreams take years to materialize, as is shown by this next story:

Betsy dreamt that she was in her car, driving home, when suddenly the radio announced that "Mark (her husband) will not be coming home tonight, or any night in the future." This message was certainly shocking. As the dream continued, she arrived home, looked around the house, and realized that all pictures of Mark had disappeared. She turned on the TV and heard the newsman say, "Beware of Secretariat." Betsy didn't know what to think. Was Mark betting on the horses? That seemed ludicrous, and she soon forgot about the dream. Everything seemed to be fine. Five years later, Mark indeed did leave home, and they were divorced. He had fallen in love with his secretary. Had Betsy taken this dream seriously and decoded her symbols, she might have been able to arrange a different scenario. (I love the play on words dreams can present: 'Secretariat,' a winning race horse, symbolized the husband's secretary. How apt.)

DREAMS OF A PAST LIFE

"I recognized you instantly. All of our lives flashed through my mind in a split second. I felt a pull so strongly towards you that I almost couldn't stop it." J. Sterling, *In Dreams*.

Reincarnation

Many searchers for truth and reason have found that reincarnation answers many difficult questions. Reincarnation proposes that your soul lives through many lifetimes, learning the lessons needed to reach the Oneness. You come back to this earth, in a new body each time, for another 'semester' in school. If you slipped a bit in one lifetime, you must work on correcting that error this time around.

For instance, in her past life Marta may have been intolerant of others who were overweight, self-righteously believing they could help themselves if they really wanted to. She may have chided them, poked fun behind their backs. This time around, however, Marta herself is grossly overweight, struggling constantly to curb her addiction to mounds of food. She must experience and feel the pain that she did not realize existed in the lives of those she previously tormented.

Dreams of Past Lives

Dreams of another life, one before your present incarnation, have a different feel and look about them. The setting is a past era; the clothing, transportation, lifestyle and culture reflect that time. You may even find yourself speaking in a language other than your current native tongue. You have remembrances or see experiences of being someone else. It is as though you are on a stage, living out a drama that is very real to you. Images are clear and crisp.

As with all dreams, these have a specific purpose. They do not come merely to entertain or to stir up curiosity, although they do both. They work as a vehicle to remind you of something important that you otherwise would not dredge up from your subconscious on your own. You most likely are struggling with a specific frustration or anxiety. You might have a path blocked or a relationship in jeopardy. The past life dream shows you where those concerns began, the source of the lessons you are now continuing to learn. Once you understand the source of your challenges, you can begin to work on them more efficiently and effectively. Let's look at some of these past-life dream examples:

As she slept, Gina stepped into feudal times where she was, due to an arranged marriage, the wife of a Lord of the Manor. She despised her husband and the conditions that gave her no opportunity to choose her mate or her life. She fervently wished she could have what she perceived to be the freedom and liberty of the serfs. At one point she was so despondent that she contemplated suicide, but could not leave her children without her love and comfort.

In this lifetime, she has freedom but has learned it doesn't always bring happiness. She chose her husband, but not wisely. Her marriage ended in divorce. Gina then remarried, after being warned about her intended's emotional limitations. She was determined to ignored those who would 'rob her of her choice' and jumped right in. She later learned that her husband, while very intelligent, had Asperger's syndrome. He lacked the ability to empathize, and could not pick up well on social cues. He tended to take things very literally. He was analytical, but not intuitive.

Gina, a demonstrative, sensitive person, found it hard to deal with the lack of communication and positive energy that she needed. Knowing the why of the problem did help, and she worked hard to make things come together. She learned to express herself in a deliberate, precise way. She now relies for the most part on her family and friends for emotional support. Gina and her husband are now a much happier, more contented couple. Gina has been given not only the freedom of choice but is learning the importance of choosing wisely.

Robert has a dream that seems to take him back in time. Everything is crystal clear:

He is riding in a horse-drawn carriage down cobbled streets. Dirt-smudged boys are energetically clearing off the horse manure. He tosses one a coin.

He sees a poor young woman with a child in arms, begging on the streets. He is startled. He recognizes her as his former parlor maid, the one he had to turn out when she announced she was pregnant, and thus disgraced. His only son later admitted she had succumbed to his charms. He cringes inwardly to realize that his first, perhaps only, grandchild is in these onerous circumstances. But there is nothing he can do. Society doesn't provide for sympathy or generosity for the fallen.

As he wakens, he wonders how this dream could possibly relate to him. He is a businessman who takes good care of his employees. He feels he is fair, although particular. Then he remembers – a single mother with little education had been hired for the mailroom. She was punctual and pleasant, but had trouble getting things right. She was trying, and with some extra help might have worked out, but he felt it was not worth the time and money to derail another employee for that task. He let her go. He remembers the disappointment and near panic in her face. Robert resolves to have his personnel department contact her and try to make things right.

From the time he was two, Ray couldn't swallow pills. There seemed to be a permanent constriction in his throat. He had a persistent cough, summer or winter.

As Ray entered his twenties, he began choking on his food. At first it was infrequent, and minor. After several years, it became a real problem. His choking became more severe; he could hardly breathe; the food was almost impossible to dislodge. Doctors could find no cause. Ray was beginning to panic. During this time Ray had a disturbing dream. He reports:

"It is a clear afternoon. I am riding a horse and approach a large house, which I realize is my home. It looks just like one of the plantation homes that existed in the old South. I am coming back early from a trip up north. I see another rider galloping away from the house. I am anxious. I fling open my door and see my beautiful wife in her bedclothes, moving languidly toward the fireplace. She sees me and is terrified. I am overcome with anger and feelings of betrayal. I then see my hands around her slim neck, choking the life out of her. When she falls, all goes black." Ray notes that this dream reappears frequently, becoming shorter and shorter, until only the anger and act of strangulation are left.

Ray has been raised to believe in God and has made all attempts to live a virtuous life. He has also been introduced to the idea of reincarnation and of karma. He decides to talk to a good friend about his current problems and about the troubling dreams. Ray's friend suggests that the dream may be a past-life memory, and that the law of karma dictates, in this case, that Ray die by the same method as did his wife in their past life together, so that Ray can understand what she went through, and requite his debt. The law, however, also provides for mercy and grace. The friend suggests that forgiveness of the old betrayal is the only path to redemption.

Ray ponders this, and prays constantly that he will have the strength to overcome his old fury. As he falls asleep a few days later, he again sees his past wife's face, and moves toward her, putting his hands around her neck. He then stops, and places his hands around her shoulders. He looks into her eyes and says, "I forgive you. Please forgive me." The dream fades.

From that time forward Ray had no more incidents of coughing or choking. He was able to live a full life. His dream had been an avenue of understanding and a venue for action that not only saved his life but mended his heart and soul.

Shawna is a talented young African American woman. She is a successful professional, well spoken, energetic and friendly. Yet she repeatedly finds herself in situations where others put her down and use racial slurs against her. She is desperate to know why these attitudes seem to follow her no matter where she goes or what she does.

One night Shawna dreams of herself as mistress of a sprawling mansion in Georgia. She wears a lace-trimmed gown; her long skirt trails the polished floor. A corset holds her stiff. Everything around her glimmers and shines. The furnishings speak of wealth and power. Her family owns many slaves, and she is proudly in charge of those in the home. She takes especial care to exercise her Christian duty and never once strikes any of the 'servants'. She is, however, quick with her tongue. She sees herself berating a young girl so severely that the girl stands sobbing, tears running down her face. 'Shawna' then curses her further for having no discipline. She sends her back to the kitchen, telling her to polish the silver again and to "get it right this time."

Shawna realizes when she wakes that she is, in her current life, experiencing the other side of the coin. She also realizes that she is still a bit rigid in her expectations. She determines to take action to rectify her misdeeds of the past. She curbs her perfectionist tendencies. She provides a training program for new employees and offers free tuition for workers who need further education to advance their careers. Shawna hires a young girl to help in her home and places her under the kind tutelage of Mercy, a trusted household manager.

It isn't long before Shawna no longer has to endure the slights and slurs that previously plagued her. She has seen the light, thanks to the eye-opening drama of her past-life dream.

ESP

"Dreams that do come true can be as unsettling as those that don't." Brett Butler.

The stress and tension of our everyday world frequently blocks our natural intuition and our creative perceptions. Influenced by our culture, we also tend to throw up an automatic defense against anything that isn't scientific, that can't be seen, touched or proven.

While in a relaxed dream state you feel safe, and can be peacefully be in touch with your subconscious. In this state you soon become aware of the natural capacity of the mind known as ESP (extra-sensory perception). Through this sensitivity, you are able to receive the thoughts and concerns of friends, family, co-workers. You are, perhaps unknowingly, in the habit of being on the same "wavelength" with those close to you anyway. When the energy of their thoughts is particularly strong and persistent, it can reach you and reflect itself in your dreams.

Megan experienced such a dream event. She had not been in touch with her friend Emmie for several years, but she dreamt that Emmie committed suicide. When she awoke, Megan immediately prayed for Emmie and continued her prayers regularly. When she was finally able to contact her friend, Megan learned that Emmie had been contemplating suicide. Emmie relayed that her deep emotional pain and depression had suddenly left her, just around the time Megan started praying for her.

This dream emphasizes the fact that, if nothing else, you can always pray for those involved in a dream that at first glance seems to be predicting doom.

In another example, Sue fell peacefully to sleep, only to dream that her best friend Nan was moving to Oregon (from California where they both currently lived). Nan seemed delighted about the move. Sue felt a bit down when she woke up; she didn't like the thought of losing her best friend, even in a dream.

Sue immediately called Nan and was greeted with Nan's excited announcement that her husband had been promoted and was being transferred to Oregon, where Nan wouldn't have to work. She had just heard this news the day before. Sue was amazed, and told Nan about her dream. Sue confessed she was upset about losing her but truly glad that Nan and her husband had this great opportunity. They decided to go out and celebrate and were determined to keep in touch. After all, they were only a state away. It wasn't as though Nan was moving to the South China Sea!

On rare occasions, you may "experience" events in great detail that happen to close friends or family:

Jeanne, in a dream state, suddenly felt a horrific fear take hold. She was in an underground parking garage, her arm heavy with the day's receipts from her boutique. She was looking into the desperate, wild eyes of a young man, dressed all in black. She started to scream, saw a flash of light, and crumpled in pain. Everything faded. Jeanne woke with a feeling of dread. She knew this dream must be about her best friend, Barbara, who had a successful shop in a local mall. She called Barb's home, and her distraught husband confirmed that Barbara had indeed been shot the night before and was in critical condition. Although she feared she would be rebuffed or seen as 'one of those', Jeanne called the authorities and told them of her dream. She described the attacker in great detail. The police recognized a man who had been arrested for violent crimes in the past; when they picked him up for questioning, he still had the bag of checks and cash in his apartment. Had they not been able to take such quick action, he might have fled the area.

People of all ages, nationalities, cultures, and religions report having such dreams. It seems that ESP, or psychic experiences, are definitely within that range of human abilities we call normal. If you have such gifts, you are not crazy, loony, or weird. We all have some ESP, in one way or another. You may sense when your sister is going to call, or when she wants you to call her. You may 'know' when a child is in trouble. For example:

Jane's father was on his way to a business meeting, when suddenly he knew he must turn around and go home. Jane was in trouble. As he neared home, he saw Jane lying on the sidewalk. A stray dog had jumped up and thrown her to the ground. He rushed her to the hospital. Had Jane's dad not decided to follow up on his intuition, who knows what might have become of Jane?

The Science: It has been determined that a decrease in melatonin is related to waking psychic experiences. When sleeping, the level of melatonin in the body drops to its lowest point during REM sleep. At that stage, you are susceptible to ESP and/or psychic dreams. Such dreams are usually triggered by the energy generated by the thoughts or emotions of those close to you.

DÉJÀ VU
"It's Deja Vu All Over Again" Yogi Berra

Feel you've seen it before, done it before? You may be recalling a precognitive dream, one that has faded from recent memory. As you approach the scene or event, your subconscious remembers the dream. Sometimes the full memory of the dream returns, even tells you what is going to happen next. If you don't like what happened next in the dream, you can then avoid the negative by changing your course.

Alternatively, it may be that you have seen the person, landscape, or building in a past life. You will sense a special energy and may even feel distant from the present moment while it all soaks in.

The television industry has appealed to our fascination with such dreams. The 'Twilight Zone', a very popular program produced by science-fiction author Ray Bradbury, originally broadcast from 1959-1964. On February 10, 1961, the show presented an episode entitled "Twenty-Two".

"Twenty-Two" tells the tale of Liz, a woman hospitalized for exhaustion due to overwork. Each night for six nights, she dreams that a nurse leads her from her room and down the hall to the elevator. The patient takes the elevator to the basement, where she sees Room 22, labeled 'The Morgue'. The nurse motions to her, saying, "There's room for one more, honey." Liz runs, screaming hysterically.

Liz is finally released and plans a trip to Miami. Her plane is number 22, and as she is about to board, the stewardess, a mirror image of the nurse in Liz's dream, tells her not to worry, and says "There's room for one more, honey." Liz runs screaming from the plane. Minutes later, while rising in takeoff, the plane explodes in mid-air.

It seems clear that Ray Bradbury himself believed in the potential of dreams to warn of coming events.

SUMMARY
"They say dreams are the windows of the soul--take a peek and you can see the inner workings, the nuts and bolts." – Henry Bromel.

So many dreams, so many types of dreams. Each dream is real, each one is personal, each one can change your life. The world of dreams is truly high adventure.

Biblical Dreams

"Pay attention to your dreams – God's angels often speak directly to our hearts when we are asleep." The Angels' Little Instruction Book by Eileen Elias Freeman.

If you like high drama, you'll love the Bible. Brother is pitted against brother, shepherds battle giants, men are thrown to the lions and survive. There is plotting, rebellion, and betrayal. Lives hang in the balance.

Interwoven into these plots, and also exhibiting high drama, are – you guessed it – dreams. There are dreams that tell the future, dreams that warn of impending danger, and dreams that save the life of a newborn babe named Jesus.

It becomes obvious that in the lives of those living 2,000+ years ago, dreams were real, dreams were personal, and dreams changed (and saved) lives.

Let's take a look at some of those long-ago dreams. Not only are they fascinating, but they reinforce everything we have learned about dreams in our own "new" age.

Joseph of the Coat of Many Colors

In the book of Genesis, we find Jacob, a patriarch of Israel, and his many sons. Joseph is Jacob's favorite. Joseph is always highly visible as he wears a special coat of many fabrics and colors. Joseph's brothers feel threatened and jealous. Joseph has a dream foretelling the future, wherein he and his brothers are binding sheaves (bundles of wheat). Suddenly and Joseph's sheaf rises up and stands upright; the other sheaves gather round and bow to his. Being young, and not exercising the best of judgment, Joseph tells this dream to his older brothers. They are not pleased. The brothers conspire against him, selling him to a passing caravan. Joseph ends up in Egypt, where he is sold again to one of the Pharaoh's officials. He then ends up in jail after being falsely accused of desiring his master's wife who actually desired Joseph, and being spurned, wreaked her revenge). [Did I tell you the Bible was full of drama, or not?]

While in jail, Joseph correctly interprets dreams for two of his companions, the king's cupbearer and baker, who had apparently somehow offended the Pharaoh (perhaps the wine had too much tannin or the bread too many sesame seeds). When the cupbearer was released and taken back to the palace, Joseph asked to be remembered. A few years down the road, the Pharaoh had a troubling dream; his magicians and wise men [notice how he kept these men on hand for just such an occasion] could not interpret it. Bingo, the cupbearer suddenly remembered Joseph, and told the king about him. Joseph was summoned, and his help "requested". Pharaoh had dreamt two dreams:

In the first dream, the king was standing by the Nile, and seven cows, sleek and fat, began to feed among the rushes. Seven other cows, ugly and lean, came up from the Nile after them, and stood beside the other cows. The ugly and lean cows ate the seven sleek and fat cows.

The second dream showed seven full, ripe ears of corn growing on one stalk. Sprouting up after them came seven meager ears, scorched by the east wind. The scanty ears swallowed the seven full ears.

Joseph first advised the king that God was the true interpreter. He also noted that since the same type of dream was presented to the king *twice*, it was because the event was already determined by God, who wanted to bring this to the king's attention so that the king could *take action*. [Take note for yourselves under similar circumstances.]

Joseph then foretold that, according to the dreams, there would be seven years of plenty followed by seven years of famine. Joseph advised the king to store up grain and charge higher taxes during the years of plenty, so the people and kingdom would not be destroyed by the famine.

Impressed, Pharaoh set Joseph up as his governor [sometimes dream interpretation really pays], and his plan was carried out. The famine came as predicted, and Joseph's brothers eventually came to him, as governor, to buy grain, bowing before him [like the sheaves in Joseph's original dream] to plead for help. Joseph eventually saves his family, and, although they had been the cause of much suffering and many trials, forgives them. He is able to see the point of his adventure in its entirety, and recognizes God's hand in it all. His journey progressed as it had so that he could now save his family from famine and thereby ensure the continuation of his people. God had promised that Jacob's line would be fruitful and multiply, and that kings would be numbered among his descendants. Joseph knew that he had played his part [which included being a dream detective] to fulfill this prophecy.

This story has it all. For you as a dreamer, it has some great information as well:

What's In It For Me?
A dream may foretell your future. Sometimes such a dream is for you alone, to prepare you, or to allow you to mediate the outcome. The dream may not be meant to be blabbed to one and all.

You are also meant to use your inner guidance when seeking the meaning behind your dream. Others may help, but you must make the final analysis.

If a dream is recurrent, it is of special import, and you must push to detect its significance. The Universe really wants you to get the message. It also wants you to take action. You are not given dreams merely for entertainment – oh, no. You must ACT on the knowledge given and the messages delivered.

Gideon the Humble Warrior
Judges (Chapter 7) relays the story of a dramatic battle:

Gideon, son of a humble farmer, was called via angelic messenger to help the Israelites escape the oppression of the Midianites. These people had created havoc for Isreal for over seven years. Gideon didn't like the idea, but when faced with direct orders and multiple signs, he gave in.

Gideon eventually pitched camp and was preparing to attack Midian with very few men. The Midians were "thick as locusts." He was advised *"in the night"* [by a dream] to steal into the Midianite camp (!!) and listen to what was being said. He was assured he would be safe. And so, being a great believer in the importance and life-changing power of dreams, he went.

As he wanders around, he overhears an ordinary soldier telling his comrade, "I had a dream: a cake made of barley bread came rolling through the camp of Midian; it reached the tent, struck against it and turned it upside down." His comrade in arms answers, "This can be nothing else than the sword of Gideon, son of Joash the Israelite. God has put Midian and all the camp into his power."

Note: We see here that it was not only the kings and wise men who knew about and believed in the power of dreams. The average "common man" apparently also took note of his dreams and discussed them with friends, who were then glad to offer their own inspired interpretations.

Gideon was very encouraged when he overheard this dream and crept back to his own camp with a much increased feeling of self-confidence.

Gideon proceeded to overcome the Midian camp with a very creative strategy. He gave each of his men a horn and a torch. During the night, they spaced out round the Midianite camp. As one, they then raised their torches while continuously sounding their horns. The Midianites panicked and fled.

What's In It For Me?

Why, you might ask, did Gideon's dream not just tell him he would win? Why did he have to sneak all the way over to the enemy camp to hear someone else's dream?

How often have you wondered if your dreams were just a reflection of your own "wishful thinking?" Or been raised from a fitful sleep only to be unable to remember your dreams? Or been unable to interpret your dreams, especially when under a lot of stress or pressure? This story shows how you can be guided by dreams of others, and by association with helpful interpreters, when you are perhaps blocked from receiving direct personal messages.

When listening to dreams of others, I am often reminded of something that has been lurking in a corner of my brain, waiting to be heard. A friend's dream may trigger an understanding of my own situation, or of a dream left untended in my journal. Sometimes I may even be blocking an interpretation because it is unpleasant – oh, yes. But when faced with another's dream that reflects my own, I am off guard. I plunge into the interpretation only to be caught up short. My heart stops. I can no longer ignore my own dream, since it's basically right in front of me!

A Slave Serves his Captor

The book of Daniel is a mini-biography. Daniel, a fine upstanding young Israelite, has, we are told, the gift to interpret dreams.

Due to unhappy circumstances, Daniel ends up in service to King Nebuchadnezzar of Babylon when the king conquers the Israelites. Time goes by, and the king has a troubling dream. He calls for his "wise men", and asks not just for an interpretation, but that they first reveal the exact content of the dream! It seems none of them are up to this near-impossible task. Daniel, however, volunteers, since otherwise all the sages would be put to death by decree of this impatient and demanding potentate. Daniel asks his friends to pray and beseech God for a revelation during the night. The King's dream, and its meaning, are then revealed to Daniel as he sleeps, and we are told that when he woke he "blessed the God of heaven."

The next day Daniel comes before the King and proclaims success, giving credit to God for revealing the mystery. He reports, "This mystery has been revealed to me, not that I am wiser than any other man, but for this sole purpose: that you the king *should learn what it means*, and that you should *understand your innermost thoughts*."

The future of the kingdom, and succeeding kingdoms, is then foretold, as revealed by the dream. The details, for the curious, are as follows:

The King, as he prepared for sleep, had been concerned about his kingdom, and about its future as it passed to others. His dream presented a statue with head of gold, chest and arms of silver, belly and thighs of bronze, legs of iron, feet part iron and part earthenware. Suddenly a stone struck the statue and shattered it. The stone that had struck the statue grew into a great mountain.

Daniel explained that the present great kingdom would deteriorate and vanish. He also promised, however, that a new kingdom would be set up by God, and that kingdom would last forever.

What's In It For Me?
The most obvious messages from this account are that:

You can pray that the meaning of a dream will be revealed

You can ask others to pray for your successful interpretation

You should learn what dreams mean

Dreams can bring you an understanding of your innermost thoughts

What is unusual in this particular story is that Daniel dreamt the exact dream as did the King. He and others were praying for this to occur, so we don't think much more about it. However, it does bring to light that two people can at times have mirrored dreams.

Mirrored dreams happen more frequently than we might imagine. Often two people who are close to each other and share each other's concerns will dream in duplicate. It is as though they are psychically tied during a period of sleep. This phenomena often occurs between sisters, mothers and daughters, best friends, close co-workers. Since women are more intuitive, dream-sharing is more prone among women, but it is not limited to women.

MORE DREAMS
Lest you think dreams went out with the Old Testament, The New Testament is also full of dream drama.

Family Matters
The story of Mary, a devout young Jewish woman, and Joseph, her fiancé, is told in Matthew (Chapters 1-2).

Joseph, a simple carpenter, was betrothed to Mary when he found she was pregnant. In those days, you did not have sex before marriage. Such behavior was scandalous, and a scarlet woman could be drummed out of her community, with no money or resources to her name, to fend for herself in an alien world. She then had few choices, none of them comfortable. Among these were suicide, to attach herself as a slave to a family outside of the community, or to become a prostitute.

Joseph, being a kind man, was going to retract the engagement informally, to spare Mary any publicity. However, "an angel of the Lord" appeared to him *in a dream*. The angel told Joseph to take Mary home as his wife, because the child within her was conceived by the Holy Spirit. The angel went even further and advised Joseph that she would have a son (they didn't have amniocentesis back then) and, cheeky angel that he was, further told Joseph what to name the boy! In those times children, especially boys, were named in accordance with family lineage. The angel, however, advised Joseph to name the boy Jesus, which meant "God is with us." This would not have been one of Joseph's choices within his cultural framework. Joseph must have been overwhelmed. But –

Did he waiver? Did he complain? Did he think he had imagined it all? No. When Joseph woke, we are told, he *did what the angel of the Lord had told him to do.* He had complete faith in the dream, knew dreams were life-changing, and *took action.* He wed Mary, and when she gave birth, named the son Jesus.

I wonder what we would have done in the same circumstances?

This was not the end of Joseph's dreams. Oh, no. Before the birth, when Mary was full-term, a decree went out from King Herod for all citizens to return to the towns of their births and register for taxes. [I guess the IRS isn't all that bad after all. They don't care where we register.] So Joseph sets out, with a single donkey, on which Mary rode, while he walked alongside. This naturally took a while. Having no cell phones, they couldn't make reservations, so when they arrived in Bethlehem, they were guided to an inn which had a clean stable on the property. It was there that Mary gave birth. Joseph must have been disappointed that they were so far from home but was pleased that the baby was perfect. While waiting for Mary to recover, they had some unusual guests from the surrounding fields. Lowly shepherds appeared eager to see the baby, claiming angels had proclaimed the event to them. Joseph must have wondered what else was in store for him in this adventure.

Meanwhile, behind the scenes, some wise men who had been awaiting this birth came from the East and went to Herod's palace asking about the infant's location. This child had been prophesied to become the "King of the Jews." Naturally, Herod didn't quite care for this idea of a possible replacement. He sent for his chief priests and scribes and asked them where this future leader of Israel was to be born, and they advised that it was in Bethlehem. Herod passed this information on to the wise men, telling them that when they found the babe, to return and report so that he too could go and pay him homage. Of course Herod actually had a more devious plan in mind.

The wise men set out, found the child, and offered gifts of gold, frankincense and myrrh. Imagine the wonderment of the two middle-class parents at these gifts fit for a king. As the wise men slept before returning to their country, they were *warned in a dream* not to go back to Herod. Knowing the importance of dreams, and believing in their life-changing messages, they *took action* and returned by a different way. It must have taken great faith to make a change in plans that meant a journey that would be longer and more difficult, and even greater faith to ignore a King of great power.

It was now just about time for Joseph and Mary to return home. I'm sure Joseph was anxious to get Mary into their comfortable home, amongst friends and relatives, where she would have help with the newborn. He must also have wanted to return to his work as a carpenter, to get busy with orders that may have fallen behind, and to provide for his family.

But what to his wondering eyes should appear? Another dream, of course. [I'm surprised that he hadn't given up sleeping by this time!] In this dream, Joseph was told *not* to go home [drats]. In fact, he was specifically told to go to Egypt with his family and to stay there until advised otherwise, because Herod was searching for the baby to do away with him. Imagine Joseph's disappointment. But did he waiver? Did he complain? Did he think he had imagined it all? Well, he might have complained a little, we don't know, but he did *take action* and go straight to Egypt. He knew with certainty that dreams are real, dreams are personal, and dreams can change your life.

Meanwhile, back at the palace, Herod was furious that he had been outwitted by the wise men. He ordered that all the male children two years of age or under, in Bethlehem and the surrounding district, be killed. I imagine that upon hearing that news Joseph was thankful he had not ignored the dream urging him to relocate to Egypt.

After Herod's death, Joseph's friendly angel appeared in yet another dream and told him it was now okay to take his family back to Israel, for those who had wanted to kill the child were now dead. So Joseph got up, packed their things, and headed for Israel. Home at last.

He headed originally for Judaea, but when he learned that Archelaus had succeeded his father Herod as ruler of Judaea, Joseph was a bit anxious about returning there. So, *warned in a dream* (which by now he knew *not* to ignore), he switched gears for the region of Galilee. There he settled his family in a town called Nazareth.

What's In It For Me?

Dreams often give you answers to questions you are currently pondering. [Joseph is given reassurance that it's okay to wed Mary.] They also may explain the situation so that the course to be taken can be understood. [Mary is impregnated by the Holy Spirit.]

Dreams can also warn of danger, and give advice as to how to avoid that danger. [Joseph is told to relocate to Egypt, immediately. The Wise Men are told to go home by a different route.]

What makes all dreams come to life, however, is not just when they are listened to; not even when the message becomes clear; but the moment when *action* is taken by the dreamer.

A Wife Warns her Husband

On the other hand, Matthew 27 relays the story of a dream that went missing:

The chief priests and elders of the Jewish community, fearful of Jesus' power and popularity, decided that He had to be removed – permanently. They trumped up the charge of blasphemy, and brought Jesus before Pilate, the Roman Governor, for trial. As Pilate was seated at the chair of judgment, his wife sent him an urgent message, "Have nothing to do with that man; I have been upset all day by a dream I had about him." Pilate, however, in the interests of politics, and against his better judgment, gave in to the crowd. We know what happened next. Pilate went down in history, not with honor, but in infamy.

Note that Pilate's wife thought her dream important enough to interrupt her husband at his place of business. Note also that he read the message. Unfortunately, that's all he did.

What's In It For Me?

Dreams of others, especially of those close to you, can at times have messages that are meant for you. It is best to listen to those as carefully as you do to your own.

IN A FEW WORDS

Regardless of the type of dream, it is always personal. A dream addresses your own life situations, relationships, and opportunities. It warns, advises, and prods. It is your constant nighttime companion.

It's finally time for you to learn how to break into this nightly world of all-knowing (and free) communication.

How to remember your dreams, including
how to train your brain!

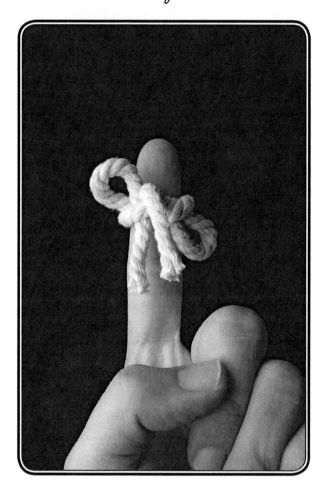

Remember Me?

"Whatever you can do, or dream you can, begin it. Boldness has genius, power and magic in it." Goethe.

Your mind is the builder. Your mind pays attention. Your mind follows orders.

What do you want? What do you need? What is on your wish list? Tell your mind.

Your desire, and your will, molds your mind.

If you want change, if you're unhappy, if you need more – tell your mind.

Your mind cooperates with you. It cooperates with your subconscious, your unconscious, your guardian angels, your spirit guides, with the Universal Forces that love you.

How does it communicate with you?

Through your dreams.

But there's a catch:

IT'S SO *HARD* TO REMEMBER!

I hear so often, "I just can't remember my dreams." You frown, you stamp your feet, and let go a big sigh. Well, of course you can't remember your dreams. You have programmed your subconscious not to do so, with all that negative moaning and groaning.

Thoughts are things: they create your words, your actions, your relationships, your world. They help you expand your horizons and talents, or shrink them into oblivion.

You must reprogram your subconscious. Every morning, every night, any time at all, think, "I remember my dreams. I value my dreams. I use my dreams." Do not say, "I *will* remember my dreams" – this puts the process in the future. You want to remember your dreams this very day – or night, as the case may be.

Once you do catch a dream, or even a snatch of one, grab your dream journal and write it down immediately. There's no shortcut. You must write your dreams down first thing when you wake up. *First thing.*

As you later scan what you've written, a few more images may pop into your mind. Write those down too.

Soon you will be filling pages and pages with your dreams. The will to do creates the ability to do!

The Science: It is hard to remember your dreams because they are stored in short-term rather than long-term memory. This is because norepinephrine and serotonin, which are necessary for long-term memory, are not being produced in REM sleep, which is when dreams occur.

If a dream is particularly vivid and you remember it upon waking, mulling it over in your mind, it may become part of your long-term memory. This often happens with nightmares, or repetitive dreams.

By immediately writing your dream down when you awake, at least part of the dream lodges in your long-term memory. Your journal then stands ready to bring the remainder of the dream to life.

TRAIN YOUR BRAIN

Rrrrrring! Rrrrrring! Your alarm jars you from sleep. In a fog, you jump up, flick it off, and try to clear the cobwebs. Wait – what is that in the back of your mind? An elusive memory floats by. Was that a dream? You wrinkle your brow in concentration. If you push hard enough ... no, it's gone, irretrievably gone. Oh, well, better get that coffee on and start the day. Maybe next time.

Sound familiar? You're not alone. That alarm clock does its job all right, which is to immediately intrude into the center of your being and pull you out into the 'real' world. To catch dreams before they're gone, you will again have to do a programming job. Just pretend you're a computer, and you'll do fine.

Your goal is to wake up about 15 minutes prior to the alarm going off. In this way, you wake up slowly and peacefully and retain your dream memories. You have time to get your dream down before you rush into the day.

This isn't as hard as it may sound. You perform a bit of self-hypnosis, so to speak. Each night, tell yourself that you will wake up at, say, 6:15. You program this into your mind, repeating the message every night until it takes hold.

If this doesn't work, try setting your alarm to ring 15 minutes earlier for one to two weeks. Then set it ahead to your usual time. We are creatures of habit. Your brain should now recognize that its new wake-up time is 6:15 and do so without benefit of that jarring alarm.

If you find you absolutely need the alarm, then keep it set 15 minutes early, recognizing when you slam it off that this is your dream time. Let no other thoughts intrude, until you get that dream down on paper. Then, and only then, let your mind drift to coffee.

You can do it.

Scientifically Blocked Memory

There is one element in dreams that almost no one can recall in detail:

You turn the corner of a quiet city street. A street sign announces its name. Even while dreaming, you know this is important. You focus full concentration on reading the name. You go over it slowly and carefully two or three times and think you finally have it. You try to burn it into your brain so that you will remember it when you wake and can then write it down.

You wake and, remembering your dream, try to bring that street name back to life. You push, prod, cry, threaten, but your mind will not bring it forth. It is gone forever. Don't worry, you're not getting senile. This is a very normal occurrence. No need to fear. That name is in your subconscious and has begun to work behind the scenes. It will do its job regardless of your faulty memory.

Why does this happen? Dreaming and reading are controlled by different brain mechanisms. Dreaming is a right-brain activity. Sometimes left-brain activities like reading or puzzle-solving, are carried across into dreams, if you are sufficiently intellectual or perhaps addicted to crosswords. This is very rare, however, and even then you often only sense that you are reading, the words being blurred or gone in a flash. It doesn't help that you tend to be severely dyslexic in your dreams – focusing on actual words and making sense of them becomes next to impossible.

So don't worry too much about road signs or words in the clouds. Use the rest of your dream to ferret out meaning and the message will be there, even without decoding the sign. Its message will blend itself into the whole.

MEMORY ENHANCEMENT
Boosting your memory can not only enhance your waking life but also helps when it comes to remembering your dreams. For those of you who would find a memory boost helpful, here are some tips:

Feed Your Brain
One of the easiest ways to increase memory power is to work specific foods into your diet.

Fish - Eat fatty fish twice a week. Salmon, albacore tuna, and mackerel are excellent sources of omega-3 fatty acids, which make brain cells more efficient. Fish eaters show a 47% less risk of dementia.

More Omega-3's - Berries, turmeric, and leafy greens all help streamline your memory.

Fruits and veggies - Use all the pretty colors – red, orange/ yellow, white, blue/purple, and green. Broccoli and cauliflower are especially potent. Include daily and you can lower your brain age by 1-2 years.

<u>Flavonoids</u> - These are antioxidants found in apples, grapes, onions, wine, tea and dark chocolate. They are great brain boosters. Not too hard to take, either.

<u>Vitamin E</u> - Avocados, olive oil, nuts and sunflower seeds are high in the antioxidant Vitamin E, which keeps the brain healthy and is especially effective at staving off Alzheimer's. Moderate amounts daily lower your risk by 67%.

<u>Other Antioxidants</u> - Oregano, cinnamon, ginger, red pepper, thyme, rosemary, and curry powder. Note: It is best to include these in food eaten at lunch time or early evening, as spices can keep your temperature up and thus interfere with sleep.

The Science: Why do they work? The brain is 60% fat. Omega-3 fatty acids DHA and EPA are crucial to maintaining brainpower. Antioxidants aid memory.

Hydrate Your Brain

<u>Water</u> - Four to eight glasses of water a day are needed to keep your brain hydrated. This helps maintain a healthy memory, and also improves the quality of your sleep.

The Science: The gray matter in the human brain is approximately 75% water. Dehydration has an extremely negative effect on brain health. Grey matter in the brain actually shrinks, and long-term dehydration can cause the brain to age prematurely.

Exercise

Physical exercise also helps you stay sharp. Thirty minutes of exercise three times a week can lower your risk of poor memory and short attention span by 20%. Doing yoga or dancelike routines is fun, too − you can socialize while you sweat. And staying connected with others doubles memory power.

Extra benefit: Studies show that adults who engage in mentally stimulating activities are 63% less likely to develop dementia.

You don't have to rush out and try to do everything on this list all at once! Just pick what looks like fun to you and get started. You'll be remembering your dreams in no time.

A GOOD NIGHT'S SLEEP

Now what, you may ask, does a good night's sleep have to do with dreams? Sleep sounds like a topic for a health clinic.

Here's the logic. To generate a solid, in-depth dream, you have to be in deep REM sleep just before waking. Tossing and turning, sleeping fretfully, throwing covers about, does not promote a sound sleep. Your dreams will be fitful and wispy. You rise ready for one thing – a good jolt of Sunrise Coffee. Dreams are not on your mind. Enter one in your journal? Forget it!

On the other hand, when you wake from a calm deep sleep, you feel fresh, alive, alert, ready to face the day. You eagerly write down the dream that you remember clearly; your mind is free of cobwebs. You thus receive the urgent message from the Universe to avoid the Toxic Table Restaurant where you would otherwise get food poisoning from the week-old mushrooms. Whew!

"And just how can I ensure a good night's sleep?" you ask. Here are some tips:

Sleep Proof the Bedroom

The *Sleeping* Room - Use the bedroom for sleep and sex only. Doing so trains your mind to associate your bed with getting zzzzs.

<u>No TV</u> - Keep the TV out of the bedroom. In fact, it's best to turn it off altogether about an hour before you intend to go to sleep. Read a good book instead.

Why is this? Let's check in on Rose:

Ah, a hot bath and a spot of brandy; now to climb under my comforter and relax all the way. Oh wait, just let me check the TV menu. I seem to remember that new crime show starts tonight…

That was fascinating. A bit disturbing, but I guess that's real life. Hmm, somehow I don't feel all cozy anymore. Maybe there's a comedy, or a talk show on – something to calm my nerves.

Morning sure comes early. I seem to remember drifting off about midnight. I must fight the desire to stay put, and push myself out of bed. I was going to start my dream journal today but oh well, maybe tomorrow.

Sound familiar?

<u>No Photos</u> – Do family photos adorn your bedroom?

Sandy, seriously ready for dreams, has her journal standing by, and even rejected a second glass of wine. Let's drop in on her thoughts:

It's only 9:00, the light's out, the bed is warm and comfy. My mind is clear of clutter. I feel sleep settling over me. I'm all set to record my dreams when the sun first streams in.

I glance up and see Mom and Dad's picture on the dresser. They look so serious. I wonder if they're disappointed in me? They had such high expectations. I love my life, I'm very comfortable, but I wonder. Could I have done better? Should I have taken another path?

Suddenly I'm not in the mood for sleep. I turn on the light and grab my murder mystery. I get totally involved and finally fall onto the pillow exhausted at midnight. Needless to say, the sun has been up a while before the alarm jars me into consciousness. No time for recording dreams now.

The lesson here? It is better to keep the family out of your bedroom. Photos make the family present, which may distract your thoughts and inhibit your sleep, not to mention your sex life. Place your favorite photos on the piano, the wall, or on your mantel, where you and others can enjoy them at leisure during the waking day.

Keep it Dark – Why? Let's see what happens otherwise:

Oh, I'm so tired. I'm just going to fall into bed and get a good night's sleep. Let me wrap this blanket around me and get nice and snug – ahhh.

Geez, that nightlight seems to be creeping right underneath my eyelids. I'll pull the blanket up a little higher.

Now I can't breathe. I'm too hot. I'm sooo frustrated. What is going on?

Duh. Why don't I simply get up and pull that nightlight right out of the wall! Yes!! Now I can relax and conk right out. Lovely.

Sleep comes, dreams come, and I am happy.

The Science: A dark room prompts your pineal gland, which is in the middle of your brain, to produce enough melatonin to help you sleep. Once you're asleep, the level of melatonin will eventually drop, so that when you reach REM sleep you can dream away.

Note: An orange light bulb (found in home improvement stores) lets you relax without inhibiting melatonin. Placed in your bedside lamp, you can safely read and still drift off when ready.

Keep It Cool – A cool room makes it easier for your core body temperature to drop, which must occur for you to fall asleep. It also inhibits the mental whirring that prevents you from drifting off. The worse your insomnia, the colder your bedroom should be. Start at 68, and go down to 65, even 60, if you still can't get any rest.

Proper air circulation and blankets that aren't too heavy can also facilitate a drop in body temperature. A hot bath may work, as afterward body temperature falls off rapidly, guiding the brain into sleep mode. Because temperature decline signals the body that it's time for sleep, turning on the electric blanket for 10-15 minutes and then turning it off may have the same effect.

Slip on some socks. Feet often feel cold because they have the poorest circulation of any body part. When your feet warm up throw the socks off and onto the floor.

The Science: When your feet and hands are warm, the blood vessels dilate, allowing heat to escape and your body temperature to fall; this initiates sleep. When hands and feet are cold, vessels constrict, retaining heat – which may keep you awake.

Check Your Mattress – You need a good, clean mattress. Dust mites can trigger asthma and allergies, causing coughing, wheezing, blowing your nose – all of which affects your sleep. Consider a replacement if yours is 7+ years old.

Personal Habits

Your daily routine can also cut into a good night's sleep.

Lots to do? - Banish worries by making a to-do list before bed, so your mind won't dwell on remembering each item while you are trying to sleep

Skip the Nightcap - A glass of wine – or two? As we listen in on Barbie's thoughts, we hear:

Oh, I'm so tired. I think I need a glass of wine.

Ummm, that tasted good. Perhaps just one more?

Oops, wait a minute. I have a homework assignment, a contract with the Universe. I want a dream tonight. I'd better stop right here and now. Another wine or two, and I'll fall asleep like I'm dead, but I know the routine. A few hours later, I'll be restlessly tossing and turning, and the morning will come all too soon, with foggy little cobwebs attached.

Sigh, I guess I'll just get a cup of decaf and one of my skinny little wafer cookies. That dream had better be a good one!

The Science: Even small to moderate intakes of alcohol can suppress melatonin, a hormone that helps regulate sleep. This then interferes with reaching REM cycles, and can prevent dreaming. For some, having a drink or two of white wine early in the evening (whatever works for you) and then switching to sparkling water, or juice, can help.

Eliminate Caffeine - Caffeine boosts alertness, activates stress hormones, and elevates heart rate and blood pressure – not helpful for a good night's sleep. Even if you've never had a problem with coffee, you may develop one over time. Age–related changes in body composition can affect the speed at which caffeine is metabolized.

For some, cutting out caffeine entirely works. You can also try having only two cups in the morning and none after 12 noon.

Switch? Try tea, which has about half the caffeine of coffee and may help calm the stress system. Green tea has about 1/3 the caffeine content of black tea. In fact, drinking 2-3 cups of green tea in the morning may actually help you sleep at night.

The Science: If you are sensitive to caffeine, its half-life (the time required by your body to break down half of it) can be as long as 7 hours. In women, estrogen may delay caffeine metabolism even further. Between ovulation and menstruation, caffeine takes about 25% longer to leave the body, and if you use birth control pills, it takes about twice the normal time.

Have a Few Carbs - An empty stomach makes it harder to fall asleep. Grab a glass of milk, a piece of whole-grain bread and butter, a banana – perhaps some chamomile tea. Do not, however, eat all the leftover spaghetti. A Real Meal will raise the body temperature and leave your eyes wide open.

The Science: Carbs boost the availability of the sleep-inducing amino acid tryptophan in the blood, which boosts serotonin, which is necessary for sleep.

Of course if you have digestive problems, eating before bedtime is OUT. Generally, avoid big meals within 5 hours of bedtime, especially anything that's highly seasoned – spices raise body temperature.

Time Your Workouts - Exercising four times a week may increase your overall sleep time by more than an hour a night. The best time to work out is late afternoon or early evening, at least two hours before bedtime, so your body temperature begins falling just as you're getting ready for bed. Relaxed exercise, such as a nice swim or an after-dinner stroll, is fine. Experiment and do what works for you.

The Science: The post-exercise drop in body temperature helps signal that it's time for sleep.

Develop a Sleep Ritual - Find relaxing activities in the evening to prepare for bedtime. It should be a nightly ritual that signals the body that it's time to unwind. It can be as simple as stepping outside onto a porch or balcony. Tidying up can be soothing: doing the dishes, putting away what you've been working on, anything that provides closure to one day and makes space for the next. One recommendation is to have a power-down hour, perhaps 20 minutes of doing things you have to finish, 20 minutes for personal hygiene, and 20 minutes for pure relaxation.

Set a Regular Sleep and Wake Schedule - Retire at the same time every evening. Your body's 24-hour rhythm, the natural ebb and flow of energy levels throughout the day, thrives on consistency. The more predictable your sleep schedule, the better your body works.

Pre-Sleep Mind Activity - To transition into sleep mode, cut off the TV and computer an hour before turning in.

The Science: Checking e-mail or scanning websites stimulates the brain, preventing you from winding down at night. Researchers at Wayne State University in Michigan found that a substantial amount of wireless signals right before bed causes headaches, difficulty falling asleep, and less restful slumber.

Go to Bed Early and Get up Early – There is an optimal time within the 24-hour clock to fall asleep and wake up. Find your cycle and stick with it. Re-train yourself if necessary. You may not get good REM sleep time if you've gone to bed late. Morning comes, the room gets lighter, your spouse gets up and turns up the heat, all while you are still trying to sleep. Not good!

The Science: Night owls are nearly 3 times more likely to experience depression symptoms than early birds, even when getting same amount of sleep. When the normal body rhythm is disturbed, sleep is disturbed, dream time is disturbed, and dream quality is disturbed. Since dreams are paramount to our good health, these disturbances may be part of the night owl's tendency to depression.

Nap Without Guilt – If the start time is before 2:00 pm, you can nap for up to two hours without impacting your sleep. A nap can even advance a good night's sleep, since sometimes being too tired actually delays your getting to sleep. Good sleep patterns mean good dream patterns.

Warm Bath and Massage – What a lovely way to nod off more easily. It also helps improve restless leg syndrome, which affects up to 10% of the population.

Keep Slim – This can help reduce your risk of obstructive sleep apnea, which interrupts sleep and causes snoring.

Medication – Prescription drugs can affect sleep. Check with your doctor; an alternative prescription may be available.

Melatonin – Tried everything and still can't sleep? This supplement causes body temperature to drop, which is necessary to fall asleep. Take up to 3 mg. of melatonin, 30 minutes before bedtime. If you can't *stay* asleep, use the time-release formula. If you experience no change after two months, stop, and see your doctor.

<u>Check for Sleep Deprivation</u> – Have you been trying unsuccessfully to sink into that deep sleep that brings those choice dreams to your consciousness? When you do get a dream, are you too tired to write it down? You may be sleep deprived. Do you recognize these signs?

1. You are hard pressed to make a simple decision
2. You eat all day and still want more
3. You have one cold after another
4. You break into tears over a love song or a re-run of "All My Children"
5. You bump into furniture and trip over the rug

There are some steps you can take during the day to help you out at night.

Morning: Get out in the sun. Walk, pull some weeds, or just sit on the porch and look around.

After Lunch: Power nap for 15-30 minutes. This will recharge your batteries.

Early Evening: Aerobic exercise is great for your body, which will cool down and be ready for a good rest later on.

All Day: Work on something interesting. Mental exercise burns a lot of energy. It perks you up at the time, and you're ready to sleep later on.

Eat for stamina: Snack on nuts, saltines, fruits and veggies through the day; have smaller meals when the time comes.

As Needed: Have some tea or coffee. Add a bit of honey for a special boost.

If you keep yourself active and awake during the day, your body will be ready to get some real rest at night. You'll be able to generate some great dreams, as well as feel ready to go in the morning.

<u>Snoring</u> - There may be another problem, however. Beware of snoring partners. Sleeping next to someone who snores throughout the night can cause serious sleep deprivation. Many couples sleep in separate rooms to resolve this dilemma. It might be that you or your partner has sleep apnea (snoring can be a symptom), for which there is a medical solution. Talk to your doctor.

<u>Especially for Seniors</u> - Seniors tend to head to bed early. The day has tired them plumb out, and they've had enough. The trouble is, if you go to bed too early, you might wake up before your REM sleep period has given you a dream hit. Here are some helpful hints to help you keep a natural rhythm to your day.

Have a quiet 'time-out' each day, all to yourself, just to relax. Meditate, watch the hummingbirds, reminisce, or think of nothing at all.

Take a 15 minute nap in the afternoon, with shades drawn. This gives you a real boost of energy, without disturbing your sleep that night.

Have dinner around 5:00 and schedule a walk, a gentle yoga session, or other activity in the *early* evening. Those who practice tai chi often sleep for nearly an extra hour a night. These mild exercises can help you drift off quickly and wake up less often.

YOU'RE READY!

OK – You have trained your brain, worked on memory enhancement, sleep-proofed your bedroom, and reviewed your personal habits. You are having dream after dream – *and* you are remembering them. Great. So what comes next?

How to record your dreams.
The necessity of immediate action.

Your Dream Journal

"Eternal vigilance is the price of liberty." [and of dreams!] **Wendell Phillips.**

DO IT NOW!
Once your dreams start rolling in, write them down *immediately* – if not sooner. Dreams fade as minutes pass.

The Science: The part of your brain which holds onto a dream is the part used for short-term memory. Once awake, your dream will fast become a mist and disappear into the daylight.

Are You Ready?
To be able to record your dream immediately, you must be prepared.

Linda was willing, but:

> I wake softly, the early morning light sifting through the blinds. My mind is full of images and muted colors. I'm still half-asleep; a dream filters into my consciousness. Ah, this is the time – I will write it all down before it escapes into the ether. I check my bedside table. Nothing. I struggle to awaken further. I open the drawer. What a jumble. I shuffle around wildly. Where is that dream journal? Where is my pen? I'd better turn on the lamp. Oh, there they are, on the floor.

> Now where was I?

Oh, yes, the dream – it's gone!

Let's take a look at Rick in action:

Rick did all his homework. He read a chapter from his dream book. He repeated his mantra, "I remember my dreams," several times throughout the day. He put a note under his pillow. His bedroom was free of light and noise. He was hopeful that this would be the night.

And it was! Close to dawn, he dreamt of light and music and messages from afar. He struggled awake and reached to turn on his lamp to write all of this down.

His arm swept upwards. Unfortunately, his bedside water bottle was in the way and crashed to the floor. The dog started howling. This woke his wife, who started glaring. By the time everything was sorted out and his lamp turned on, the dream had flown right out the window – along with a peaceful day.

On the other hand, Brenda, an equally conscientious dreamer, went to bed equally prepared. Brenda, however, had a "touch-on" lamp, which gives light at the one-two-three tap of a finger. When the time came, Brenda simply tapped the shade of her lamp once and a soft glow appeared. Her water was safe, her dog and husband still asleep. She reached for her dream log and pen (which had been placed close at hand), peacefully scribed her message from the night, and went back to sleep.

This all sounds great, you say, but my bed partner is extremely sensitive to light. I don't think even a touch-lamp would help. A flashlight is one alternative. Sneaking into the bathroom is yet another technique. You can keep your pen and journal in the magazine rack!

More Helpful Hints

Before going to sleep, use the notepad (or iPad) beside your bed to jot down the date and three or four lines about what you did and how you felt that day.

As soon as you are awake, before you get out of bed, think backward. Ask "What was just going through my mind?" Jot down anything, a little piece of a dream, a solitary image or feeling, or just the fact that your mind was blank. Simply writing down a line or two each day will enhance your ability to remember. You are almost always dreaming just before you wake; soon you will be able to remember plenty of dreams.

Don't worry if you don't remember a full dream every day. One or two a week will keep you busy as you start working with your dreams.

Your Dream is Recorded – Now What?

As you go through your morning, ponder the dream. Refresh your memory by looking over your notes. As you move throughout the day, let your mind glide over your dream, so that your intuitive, subconscious self can begin helping you out. When you have a few moments to yourself, give it your complete attention and try to unlock its secrets. (More on the interpretive process later.)

THE *WHOLE* DREAM?

I sense that you have a question. What might that be?

"Well, you have advised me to write my dream down right away. How detailed do I have to be? Do I have to include every little thing? That might take a long time."

You're right, at first it might take a long time. As you get used to the process, however, your dreams will get shorter. They won't have to crowd in as much information to get through. You will recognize symbols and threads of meaning more quickly. Your dreams can stop going on and on in an effort to get in as many hints as possible in hope that you will pick up on at least one or two of those hints.

Meanwhile, jot down as much as you can possibly remember. Sketch out the dream story itself; include colors you remember, scents, voices, emotions. Note how you felt when you woke up.

Draw a picture of anything that seemed unusual in your dream. For example, if you saw an odd-shaped cloud floating in the sky, draw the cloud in your journal. A week later, the words "odd shape" might not have much meaning.

Avoid an immediate comparison. When you see a tall, steel, lattice-shaped tower in your dream, you might be tempted to say you dreamt of the Eifel Tower. In reality, it may be representing part of the power station just down the street. Of course, it may also symbolize the Eifel Tower, but initially a good description will do.

The more you have to work with, the more accurately you can interpret your dream, and the more benefit you will receive from it. The more effort you put in at the beginning, the easier it will be down the road. Don't get lazy! You want to become a dream virtuoso.

EVERY DREAM?

Bob would wake at 2 a.m. with a vague memory. It would take 15 minutes to recall and record his dream and another 30 minutes to get back to sleep. Bob was just getting started with his dream journal and didn't want to lose track of any of his dreams. At the same time, he needed to get a full 8 hours in before heading off to work. He decided to try a new technique. He would record the bits and pieces that came immediately to mind, then slide back to sleep.

This is a good technique, and it's easy to use. Merely jot down whatever images come to mind immediately. Don't worry about the sequence, or details, or about getting everything just right. Stay in your fog. For example, you might write "white horse, sunset, crickets chirping, anxious." When you are fully awake in the morning, check your notes, and the dream will almost always flesh itself out. You can then document the remainder of the dream and go get your coffee.

Eventually, you will be able to program your dreams to materialize just before you wake up, and you'll have no more worries about interrupted sleep. Dreams cooperate with your subconscious, which cooperates with your needs, as instructed!

I was initially waking up 4-5 times a night with one dream after another. I finally said, "Hey, Universe, please just have my most important dream presented to me right before I wake up in the morning. I absolutely *must* get my sleep." And sure enough, that's what happened.

Persistent Dreams
Certain dreams stay with you whether you choose to write them down or not. These dreams are so potent and full of emotion, so frightening and so compelling, that when you wake, you remember them vividly. You pore over them. They then become stored in the part of your brain that gives you long-term recall. This type of dream is usually recurring, which reinforces memory to an even greater degree. Such dreams are very meaningful and ripe with helpful information and guidance. They keep coming until you unlock the message and take action.

IS IT WORTH ALL THIS FUSS?

This dream better be worth it, you say to yourself. I got up early just so I could write it down. You read it over, amused that the musical scale being played in your dream was initially very flat and dull. You booed; the pianist laughed, then started up a lively little tune.

You peek at the clock and see that it's time for coffee. Meanwhile, you mull the dream over in your mind's eye. You begin to put together threads of meaning. As you pour that dark liquid into your cup, you get an 'aha' moment. Wow. That meeting you have today. You're going to have to inject some humor into your little pep talk so as not to hurt any feelings and fall flat on your face. Thanks dream! This might help bring on another "well done" from Mr. Bigbucks.

EXTRA, EXTRA, READ ALL ABOUT IT!

"Look at a stone cutter hammering away at his rock, perhaps a hundred times without as much as a crack showing in it. Yet at the hundred-and-first blow it will split in two, and I know it was not the last blow that did it, but all that had gone before." Jacob A. Riis.

Dream Journal "Extras"

"Dream Journal extras? My goodness!" I hear you say. "Isn't pulling the essence of a dream out of my head and getting it on paper enough?"

Well, that is a good start. You can't do anything without the dream, that's for sure. However, I know you want to get the most out of all your hard work and productive dreaming. Here are a few 'extra' tips:

1. Before you go to bed, grab your journal and log in the date and day of the week. This provides a useful reference

point when you review your dreams. It can also help connect a series of dreams. Also jot a brief summary of your day's concerns, challenges, successes, whatever is claiming your current energy. This will help your interpretive efforts later on.

2. After you wake and log in your dream, note (a) whether it was a middle-of-the-night dream, a nap dream, a just-before-the-alarm-clock-rang dream, and (b) the mood you were in when you woke up. Your mood is always a clue for unlocking the dream message.

If you can't remember the whole dream, don't give up. Log in the body of the dream: the scenes, locations, characters, animals, major objects, major colors, the mood. Any little thing you can remember is fine. The more you practice and stick to your routine, the more you will remember and the more you will understand. Dream work is just like learning to ride a bike, play the piano, understanding long-division. Sorry.

Advanced Dream Journal Extras (Optional)

Computer Magic: - Some energetic people take dream images and related information from their Journal and input the data into a computer. (Related information includes daily events, issues, emotions.) These dream scientists are then able to scan quickly for patterns and relationships between dream content and what's happening in their waking lives.

Constant Comment - You may remember a dream or get an 'aha' moment as you are driving down the road, shopping for groceries, waiting for an oil change. It is then that you whip out your pocket-sized notebook and make notes. (If you have been driving down the road, I suggest you pull over first.) You later transfer these notes to your Dream Journal. A lot of work?

You will be surprised. As you recall more, your motivation, interest, and intuition will increase; your life will benefit. You will become addicted to dreams and their life-changing beauty. You will be thrilled when you have the opportunity to whip out that notebook.

Waking dreams can also be recorded in your handy pocket notebook. Perhaps you have been trying to decide whether or not to get a puppy. As you travel down the road, you hit all the red lights. Every single one. The Universe is probably telling you that now is not the time for a puppy. Make a quick note, "(date) – all red lights – puppy."

Let's say you put the puppy off and arrange to have your deck and surrounding lawn fenced in. You still want that puppy, but you remain patient. Once more you are rolling down the road, and realize that this time you are making good time: all the lights, every single one, have been green. You again note this in your little notebook. As you make the entry, the light dawns. Now the puppy will have a safe place to play outside. Bingo. Your patience, and your attention to your waking dream, have paid off.

Review of Your Journal - Do you read a dream, try to interpret it, and then put it on the shelf, going on to new and better dreams? You may not realize it, but some of those new and better dreams may be connected to those old forgotten dreams.

A review of your journal now and then can be very helpful. As you go back, you may recall a new image or remember a sad feeling. Jot these memories down next to the dream. They may not only provide a fuller interpretation of your old dream, but you may see a thread that runs through both the old dream and some of your newer dreams. Your studious interest also reinforces your ability to get the most out of your dream work. For example:

Dottie was working on a current dream that placed her at a bank, cashing a large check. She stuffed it in her purse and walked out without a care. In reality, Dottie was struggling to make ends meet. As she perused her dream journal, she came across a dream she had entered the week before. In that dream she had picked up her mail and found a sweepstakes entry from a company called "Argonauts Inc." She had been puzzled.

As Dottie read over her journal, the light dawned. She had applied for a new job at a shipping company. It would mean a large increase in salary, but she would have to move. She was undecided. Now, reading her journal, she saw the message loud and clear. The job was undoubtedly a chance for her to get ahead. She took the job, was successful, got promoted, and struggled no longer.

WHATS NEXT?

You're on a roll. You can remember your dreams and have a fine dream journal started. Now you want answers. What are those dreams telling you? What juicy messages are they sending your way?

Let's find out how to find out.

A dream interpretation manual, just for you.

Putting It All Together

"Dreams say what they mean, but they don't say it in daytime language." Gail Godwin.

Okay, you're convinced dreams are important. You have trained your brain to remember your dreams. You now record them faithfully in your dream journal the moment you awake. What comes next?

After all this effort, you want to know what these dreams mean. What messages do they have for you? What secrets do they hold? How will they change your life?

Dream interpretation starts with a four-step overview:

1. **The Type of Dream.** What type of dream have you just had? What area of your life is the dream addressing?

2. **The Symbols.** What or whom do the symbols in your dream represent?

3. **The Action.** What is going on? Where does the dream take place? How are the characters interacting? How do you feel about it all?

4. **Your Life.** How do the symbols and action relate to what is happening in your personal life? Are you having

127

problems with relationships, money, your job? Do you have questions that seem to have no answers?

Coordination of these four elements should bring enlightenment. It is then up to you to *act* upon your dream. This final step is the first step toward changing your life.

Let's get into more detail.

TYPE OF DREAM
"Just let awareness have its way with you completely." Scott Morrison.

Basic Dream Categories
As a human being, you are three-tiered. You operate via body, mind, and spirit. When these parts of yourself are in balance, you feel great. When one dominates, there is discord and lack of harmony. You become skewed. Your three parts are not cooperating. Dreams attempt to bring you back into balance and therefore back to a happier state of being.

It makes sense, then, that a dream will address one (or more) of these parts of yourself. A dream may concern either (1) your physical body, or (2) the life activities and concerns on which your mind is focused, or (3) your spiritual life, sometimes bringing messages from a guardian angel or a departed loved one. How do you know which part of yourself is being targeted by your dream?

The Body
Dreams about your body and its health are usually in *black and white*. These dreams generally involve little or no emotion. The symbols are easily decoded.

You may see four glasses of water on your counter, indicating that you should drink at least this much water each day. You may see some dirty windows, indicating your eyes need attention. You may see a table heaped with fruits and vegetables, all looking delightfully fresh and desirable – I'm sure you'd know what that means!

The Mind

Dreams that look like a *tinted photograph*, with light washes in color, are normally concerned with the mental side of your life. These dreams may bring suggestions about a troubling problem at work, your writer's block, or even how to organize your household.

The symbols in these dreams are often manufactured objects, such as houses, carpets, pictures, money, automobiles, dishes, locks, and keys. The dream usually relates to an external problem involving some marital, social, economic, creative, or other concern requiring adjustment or needing clarification. Your mind has probably been chewing over these challenges for a while.

The Spirit

When dreams begin to come in *color*, they usually bring spiritual messages. The dream symbols are often taken from nature: animals, mountains, water, clouds, wind. Such a dream typically relates to a struggle you're experiencing with your inner self. It is about your attitude, development (or lack thereof), happiness, purpose, or ideals. The dream may give you advice, encouragement, or enlightenment.

A Combo?

Often, a dream may combine two of these categories, or even include all three. You may really have to work on that one! Of course, since your mind influences your emotions which influence your body, it is logical that at times your dreams will address all these parts of yourself. As you learn to interpret your dreams you will see the patterns clearly and it will be a piece of cake – sometimes angel food, sometimes devils food...

Caution:

Note the words *usually, normally, and generally.* Unfortunately, there are no hard-and-fast rules when interpreting dreams. If you are still unsure about the meaning of your dream after checking out colors and symbols, and perhaps soliciting a friend or group for help, you can ask to have the dream shown again in terms you can understand. Just say, "Hey, subconscious, I can't hear you. Speak up!"

Once you know which area of your life your dream is targeting, it's time to look at the specifics of your dream.

DREAM SEQUENCE
"The whole is more than the sum of its parts." Aristotle.

The opening scene presents the setting and expresses the mood, feelings, or ideas triggered by your day's residue or your life's concerns. As you move into mid-dream, the initial theme is further developed. The scenario may include both past and present experiences. The dream's end shows a proposed resolution. You then continue in your normal sleep cycle. When the resolution is unsuccessful, or not desirable, it leads to awakening.

IDENTIFYING THE DREAM ELEMENTS
"Divide each difficulty into as many parts as is feasible to understand it." René Descartes.

Dissecting your dream allows you to focus not only on the overall dream, but on the individual parts as well. As you delve into each part of your dream and discern its symbolic meaning, you will be able to connect this information to the dream's overall message. You will then be able to make the further connection to your personal life. Ask yourself:

1. What is the setting?
2. Identify the symbols:
   a. Who/what are the main characters? These will usually be people and/or animals.
   b. What objects appear in your dream?
3. What feelings did you experience while dreaming? Upon awakening?
4. What major action took place?

The Setting

The setting is never coincidental. It sets the tone, and indicates the part of your life on stage in the dream. To best understand the meaning of the setting, describe it as though you are talking to a Martian. A Martian has no knowledge of any earthly structures or objects, what they look like, how they are used, what purpose they have.

For example, if your dream takes place at an elementary school, you would make note that many young beginning students meet for instruction at an elementary school, which is usually close to where they live. They attend this school for a certain number of years. They learn the basics. Thinking in such detail facilitates your interpretation of the setting and its symbology as it relates to the remainder of your dream.

Also ask such questions as:

1. What is this place like?
2. Is it different than the same setting I am/was familiar with in my waking life?
   a. How?
3. How does it feel to be there?
4. Why am I there?
5. What action takes place there?

6. If a building, what type is it, what condition is it in, where is it located?
7. Does the setting remind me of any situation or area in my waking life?
   a. How so?

The Symbols

Symbols that appear in your dream are personal. They are yours and yours alone. The first question to ask when analyzing a dream symbol is, "What does that symbol mean *to me?*" Not to my neighbor, or to my mother, or even to the author of a dream dictionary – but to *me, myself, and I.* For example, a flower garden is usually a beautiful, pleasant sight, uplifting to the spirit. If, however, your mother spent all her time and energy on her flower garden, ignoring you and all else, you might feel resentment on seeing a large ornate flower garden.

This leads to the question, "Where do dream symbols come from?"

Sources of Dream Symbols

The mind is a vast reservoir, an endless storehouse, and an infinite computer. Day after day it stores away impressions received through your five senses. Your subconscious loves sifting through these impressions. It uses the handy symbols provided by the experiences in which you have been immersed to communicate with you in your dreams.

The Day's Activities. The majority of dreams relate to everyday life. Your hopes and dreams, cares and worries, personal and business relationships, all star in your nighttime dramas. They are accompanied by commentary, advice, consolation, enlightenment – whatever is needed to be of help at the time.

You may be considering leaving your current job for better pay, although you love the job. You then dream that you are sitting in your manager's office, at his desk and in his chair. You take this as an omen, and decide to wait things out. Within six months, you really are in that manager's office, having been promoted when he moved to Pango-Pango.

The Media. What movies or TV shows do you see? What do you read? Images, actors' names, story lines, settings, and themes are all right there to provide symbols for your nightly dreams.

An old *Star Trek* episode involving a Klingon rebellion might filter into your dream to let you know you are feeling rebellious toward your boyfriend, who is becoming too 'clingy'.

Daily Observations. Every day you notice myriads of tiny little details. You don't think about them; they just pop unbidden into your subconscious mind. They stir around in the back of your mind, ready to appear in your dreams at a moment's notice.

As you drive down the road, you see a home for sale. Your eye catches sight of a crack in the foundation, but your mind skips right over it. That night, your dream brings the memory of this scene back to you, except that this time the cracked foundation is under your own home. You realize that you have been neglecting your domestic responsibilities in favor of work, golf, and Las Vegas. You resolve to put your affairs in better order and shore up your personal foundation.

Religious Symbology. Your religious heritage is an important source of dream symbols. The devil, apple, snake, mountain, cross, Star of David, et al – each has a specific spiritual meaning for many. For example, let's say you are a Christian, and feel great stress as you care for your aging parents. You then dream of a cross glowing in the heavens; you feel encouragement and peace. When you awake, you realize that your "cross" is only temporary, and is part of your soul's journey.

Childhood Memories. Childhood experiences, especially those with emotional impact, become part of your dream language.

Your love for 'Lassie' translates your dream dog into a symbol for companionship and faithfulness. Conversely, a former traumatic experience with an angry, snarling dog may convert your dream dog into a symbol of danger and fear.

Feelings
Dreams reflect current issues in your life and are excellent emotional barometers. Dreams even affect what mood you're in when you wake up. Ever hear the old saying about waking up on the wrong side of the bed?

The absence or presence of fear, joy, puzzlement, anger, or other emotions in your dreams help point you toward the message and its solution.

For example, did you look into your dream mirror and not recognize whom you saw there? Were you puzzled and concerned? It may be that you don't recognize yourself lately. You have been acting out of character. You have been drawn into office drama and intrigue, your spiritual ideals forgotten. Get out that Windex and clean that mirror up!

What Took Place?
You've just experienced a dramatic dream. You've been the audience of one at a play produced just for you. Review the script. Why did it happen at night? Why were you being chased? Who

was chasing you? Were you angry? Was there any resolution? Have you had this same dream before?

What Does It All Mean?

Now comes the crux of the matter. What is going on in your personal life? How does the dream address these issues? Do you feel that you are in the dark? Do you feel that you are being plagued by unrealistic expectations? Are you angry about this? Can you turn around and confront your pursuer? Who is this pursuer? Is it perhaps your own ambition?

Taking Action

Now that you have determined the area of your life the dream is targeting, the meaning of your symbols, reviewed the story-line, and discovered how all these things relate to your personal life, it's time to make use of all that information.

You might decide, after being "chased" by a green monster, who turned out to be your very own driven self, to slow down a bit, to modify your ambitions, and to take one thing at a time. Perhaps to analyze what you really want out of life.

The important thing is to take action. If it's wrong, you'll get another dream. If it's not enough, you'll get another dream. The Universe wants you to succeed. If, however, you don't take action, you will get the same dream, in one form or another, until you get the message and do take action. Dreams don't like to be ignored.

DETAILED EXAMPLES

"Oh, I've had such a curious dream! said Alice." Lewis Carroll.

Now that you have the basics down, let's see how it works in greater detail:

Name That Dream

Every dream has a theme. Once you have taken the initial steps and given your dream a good once-over, try giving your dream a title, as you would a short story. This will help you determine the main, overall theme.

Sue dreamt of her old boss, who was attractive and intelligent, but controlling and a bit short-sighted. She didn't feel she could thrive in that environment, so went on to another company. In her dream, her old boss was kissing her. She was quite surprised.

She named her dream *Revisiting the Past*. As she thought about how this might tie in to her present life, she realized that her new boyfriend was a lot like her old boss. She had suppressed her feelings of disquiet because he was so good looking and charming. She now realized that she must go on to other "company" because she would not be happy in the long run with a man who wanted to program her life.

You sometimes become so engrossed with the details of a dream, that you can't see the forest for the trees. There is often such a maze of symbols, of action; scenes fade in and out. It is easy to become confused. You shake your head, and say, "What in the world is this all about?"

Leila had just such a long rambling dream, which combined three scenarios. She starts out in a sunny field, bird watching. She then drifts to a friend's home where every room is bright, and strange music comes from nowhere. From there, she ends up in a market, where all the merchandise is kept in well-lit cases. The manager comes over with a key to help her with her choices.

Again, a good tool with a dream like this is to give it a title. To do this, Leila had to search for the common thread, or most outstanding feature, of the dream. This particular dream features light in each section. The dreamer is in a sunny field, a bright room, and observes well-lit containers. Leila entitled this dream *There is Light* with a subtitle *I Can See*.

Now Leila could look back over her dream with more focus and understanding. She asked herself, "What do I see? What do I hear? What do I want to eat?" One thing she did know was that there was enough light.

Leila continued with her interpretive study. Birds are small parts of nature, colorful, and give us song. Leila noted that she was alone here. Her friend's home (her life in the community) is light and full of music. The market, a place where food is available for multiple persons, has well-lit cases. The manager (an authority figure, perhaps a guardian angel, an advisor) hands her a key to help her with her choices. This is very important. It means she can make her own choice as to which 'food', be it physical, mental, or spiritual, she wants to use for sustenance.

Leila has a beautiful voice, but has been hesitant to pursue a career in that field, since it seems so uncertain. The dream is pointing out that she has the light and the support she needs, she just has to make a choice. The light is there for her personally, for her in her community, and for her if she chooses to use her talent for a larger audience.

Did she unlock a case? More than one case? What would you have done?

Personal Symbols
"We have all a better guide in ourselves, if we would attend to it, than any other person can be." Jane Austen.

Our dreams are colored by our life's experiences. They bring us symbols that speak to us in our own unique language. A dog, for example, would initially seem to be a familiar and almost universal symbol, easily understood. However, as we delve into the following three dreams, each featuring a dog, we realize that a dog can represent a variety of qualities and emotions that are as individual as the dreamer.

Example 1

Dream One. Sarah dreams that a strange dog is on her lawn. It has no tag. She approaches it slowly, her hand outstretched; its tail wags non-stop, it sniffs her hand, then licks her face. She reassures him with a gentle pat.

Dream Two. Tom also dreams of a strange dog on his lawn. It has no tag. Tom stays on the porch. His stomach clenches into a tight ball, sweat breaks out on his forehead, and he takes a step back. He thought his old fear had flown, but here it was again. Suddenly he could smell the emergency room from ten years ago, see his ragged arm being stitched. But this is unreasonable, he tells himself. The dog that attacked him then was not this dog. This visitor looks harmless, even cute. Just then, though, the dog bares his teeth. He doesn't growl, just shows those sharp canines as though waiting, biding his time. Tom retreats into the house and calls the animal shelter.

Dream Three. Mandy too sees a dog on her lawn, with no tag. She is impressed by the dog's size and stance. The dog looks strong and capable. "This dog would undoubtedly make a good guard dog," Mandy thinks. "In fact," she muses, "he looks very similar to the seeing-eye dog Uncle Steve once had." The neighbor's dog chooses that moment to bound across the driveway to say hi. Mandy braces herself, but the unknown dog merely turns to face the interloper, staying alert but calm. Mandy is impressed.

As it turns out, each of these dreamers is dating someone on a regular basis. They are each wondering about the friend's potential for a special relationship.

In dream one, Sarah receives reassurance that her special friend, who is unattached (no tag), is indeed the friendly, loving person she has believed him to be.

In dream two, Tom is receiving a warning. His old fears are apparently not unfounded, although at first glance they seem unwarranted. The dog gives no clues, is not aggressive, but does show those teeth that lie in wait. Tom must subconsciously suspect that his girlfriend has aggressive tendencies that she has curbed thus far. He is being shown that his intuition is correct and to beware.

In dream three, Mandy realizes that she primarily seeks a relationship with someone who will protect and take care of her. She wants guidance and security. It appears that her current friend is just that type of person. He will do the job without being overbearing (the dog in the dream is not aggressive with the neighbor's pet, just watchful).

If these dreamers, seeking to interpret their dreams, had casually grabbed a dream dictionary and looked up "dog," they would undoubtedly have found such terms as "loyal, friendly, true-blue, gives unconditional love, etc." While this might have worked for dreamer number one, you can see that it would not have been at all accurate for dreamer number two, and only marginally helpful to dreamer number three.

You are special. Your life is unique. Your experiences are yours alone. You must till your own fields of memory and emotion as you search for meaning in your dreams. Ask, "What does this symbol mean to *me*?" It may take a while. That's ok. You don't want a quick fix; you want quality. You don't want to be left asking, "Where's the beef?"

This is all great, you say, but how do you get from the asking to the answer? In detail, please.

Okay, fair question. Using the same three dream examples, here is a suggested step-by-step process:

How to Get From Here to There
As the dreamer, focus on the primary aspects of the dream:

The Environment – The lawn, at the dreamer's home.

The fact that the dog is on the lawn of the dreamer's home gives a hint that the dream is domestic in nature. The dog does not appear at a park, a school ground, or on the road. This indicates that the dream is likely to be exploring the dreamer's personal life or relationships.

It is significant that the dreamer comes out of his house to observe the dog. His house is his comfort zone, his home, and his protection from the world. It can also represent his body.

The Symbol – A dog.

We then turn to the dog. What is a dog? A dog usually appears in our lives as a pet. It has, however, evolved from the wolf. It has instincts to protect itself, its pack, and its territory. As a domesticated pet, it is generally loving, obedient, friendly, protective, and loyal. It can, however, be trained to be aggressive. If it feels threatened, or its territory is being invaded, it can attack. It can also be trained to be of practical benefit to man – a guard dog, seeing-eye dog, police dog. Each dreamer must ask himself what a dog means to him, personally. As you can see in the above dream examples, this can vary greatly.

Life Circumstances – What is going on in the dreamer's life right now?

Each dreamer is in a personal relationship. There is a question in each mind as to the potential outcome of the relationship. Once the dreamer sees this particular drama as being central to his life at the time, he then asks himself several more questions.

Question One: Does the symbol of the dog represent a part of himself? If that does not seem probable, he then asks …

Question Two: Does the symbol of the dog represent anyone who is currently a part of his life?

As the dreamers turn their minds to their current relationships, they realize that the dog does indeed represent qualities or characteristics found in their current "significant others." They then begin to understand the nugget of meaning found in their respective dreams, draw conclusions, and take indicated actions.

Some dreamers, at their peril, ignore such information, later wishing they had taken it to heart. We all have choices to make. Dreams can only give us a 'heads-up'. But not to worry. We can learn from our mistakes and are always given more chances and more information.

Example 2
I myself had a dream I found quite exciting:

I saw a new red sports car waiting for me! I never had a sports car, much less a red one. Early in life, my cars were cheap clunkers.

I then turned to dependable and thrifty Hondas, Subarus, and Toyotas. I now have a Hyundai. The colors have been brown, blue, white, and silver. Now, however, I was at a new plateau. I was going to experience the long awaited "life after 60." Perhaps this sports car was saying, "This can be you. Take me for a ride. See what you think, how you like it." I became the sports car. I zipped around corners, safely of course, but definitely in a flashy manner. I felt powerful. People turned to look and to admire. I had plenty of energy, the gas supply was magical and inexhaustible. It was great.

I had no idea what was in store, but the unexpected magically unfolded and I became a published author at age 65. It felt great. I still have the Hyundai, but I'll always have the red sports car in my dreams.

Note:In this dream the color red definitely symbolized energy, especially mental and creative energy. For some, red signals sexual energy, while for others it spells danger, or an order to STOP (as in red light). Then again, if you witnessed a fatal automobile crash at an early age, involving a red car, or where blood was spattered on the road, red may signal death; for you, red is an ominous symbol. All symbols are first and foremost personal.

Example 3

Carly had repetitive dreams in which she was a spy, running from another spy who was an enemy agent. The pursuer was out to kill her. She finally knuckled down to interpret these pursuing dreams. What do spies do, she asked herself? Well, spies gather and protect secrets. They sometimes lie to cover their identities. The light dawned.

Carly realized that she herself tended to be secretive. She was sometimes not quite honest with her husband about what she was doing, how much she was spending, or where she was going, although it was all fairly innocent. She wanted to avoid confrontation. The secrets were chasing her and were eventually going to be her demise if she didn't change her approach. She decided to get out of the spy business and was never in that kind of dream danger again. To top it all off, when she confessed, it turned out her husband wasn't even worried about her habits. He knew her well enough to know she would never go off the deep end. He usually gave his blessing to her plans.

Note: We see in this dream that Carly's pursuer was actually herself.

PEOPLE IN DREAMS

"*When solving problems, dig at the roots instead of just hacking at the leaves.*" Anthony J. D'Angelo, *The College Blue Book.*

Dreams often provide you with a whole cast of diverse players. You meet strangers, friends, old school mates, lovers, spouses, technicians, firemen, judges, celebrities – it would take up less space to include those you don't meet!

The great majority of the time, each person symbolizes either a part of yourself or of someone who is currently involved in your life. To get at the heart of things, you start by asking a series of questions about the person.

1. What characteristics do I attach to this person?
2. What is his/her personality
3. How do I feel about this person?
    a. Do I like or dislike this person.
    b. Does the person upset me?
    c. Do I enjoy being with this person?
4. What is/was my relationship to this person?
5. What job does the person have?

6. What is the person's attitude toward life and others?
7. What kind of clothes, car, house, pets does this person have?
8. What is the person doing in my dream?

You will undoubtedly think of many more questions you can ask to flesh out the person in your dream.

Once you have the answers to these questions, you may recognize a part of yourself immediately. You can then reflect on the meaning of the dream by plugging yourself into the drama as an "understudy" who has taken over the role of Grandma, Sarah, or Marilyn Monroe in your dream. This can bring enlightenment in a hurry.

On the other hand, you may recognize the qualities – hitherto perhaps blocked from your conscious mind – of a girlfriend, co-worker, or repairman. The dream may be pointing out to you that a relationship is unstable; that you need to be more sensitive; or that you need another estimate. The information brought to you by your dream may open your eyes and show you the path to action, improvement, and/or success.

Of course, there are times when the person in your dream is just who he appears to be. The dream image then is usually quite sharp, and the person's appearance lifelike. The person walks, talks and looks just like Mom, or Pete, or Julia. That very real person may communicate a concern or a desire, give you advice, or just want to have some time with you, if only in your dreams.

Let's look at a few examples:

Example 1

Brad dreams of a former schoolmate, Gwen, who was in his drama class. She was always given a key role. She would strut through the school like a queen, and bestow the favor of her glance only upon the chosen few. She did have talent, but oh, what a pain. In Brad's dream, Gwen was again in the limelight, up on stage posturing and dramatically waving her hands about. Her understudy, sitting beside Brad, whispers that she hopes Gwen will forget her lines and make a fool of herself. Brad thinks that is a bit harsh, but certainly empathizes.

As Brad reads over his dream, he realizes that a recent promotion at work has made him a bit of a prima donna. He is acting a lot like Gwen used to, in fact. He senses that his friend and co-worker is thinking less of him, and may be secretly awaiting his downfall. Brad promises himself to shape up, get back to work, and seek the cooperation of those around him.

Example 2

Sarah dreams of George, an old boyfriend from years ago. They were at a restaurant and he had ordered for both of them, assuring her that his choices were the best the chef had to offer. The fact that she didn't particularly care for quail did not seem to faze him. When the waiter came over with drinks, George thought he paid a bit too much attention to Sarah, and asked for someone else to serve them.

Upon waking, Sarah remembers that she eventually broke off with George because he was too controlling and jealous. She then thinks of Robert, her current boyfriend. She has been so mesmerized by his good looks and charm that she hasn't given much thought to the rest of him. She now realizes that he has a lot of the same qualities as George. She does not want to go through that kind of experience again. She decides that she must let him go now, rather than wait for the other shoe to drop.

Example 3

Bill dreams of his best friend, Tom. Bill has moved to the east coast; Tom still lives in California. Bill misses Tom but has been so busy getting settled that he hasn't called or e-mailed him for ages. In the dream, Tom looks just like his old self, except that he is much thinner.

Bill ponders the dream. What does Tom symbolize? He thinks of Tom mainly in terms of friendship. Ah, the light dawns. Tom is thinner, and the friendship is thinner, due to lack of nourishment. Bill heads for the phone.

Example 4

Kate enters a quiet room and sees her mother and daughter sitting and talking comfortably. Kate's mother died four years ago, but Kate does not feel any surprise. Her mom and daughter always got along beautifully and loved each other with great strength. Kate sits down, and they all chat. Mom then speaks directly to Kate, and tells her, "I will be there to help you through the tunnel." Kate knows this is the tunnel of light that those leaving the earth are believed to see as they head toward the world of spirit. Kate is pleased and comforted. Her daughter then says, with a twinkle and wry smile, "I'd help you, Mom, but you know I hate that tunnel." Kate laughs.

Kate realizes that this has been a true visitation. Both Mom and daughter looked so natural and lifelike, their gestures and voices as they always were. Kate will not be afraid when the time comes to leave the earth. She hopes it is not soon, but realizes that time means nothing to those not in the material world, so doesn't worry.

STEP INTO A STARRING ROLE!
"Only those who will risk going too far can possibly find out how far one can go." T.S. Eliot.

One fun method of dream interpretation is to become one of the characters in your dream. You step into the shoes of that person/ animal/plant/doughnut. You become the object and talk to the dreamer. You explain yourself, as the symbol, to yourself, the dreamer.

This technique works especially well if you have a lively imagination, can shut down the activity of your conscious mind for a minute or two, and let your intuitive forces take over.

I will give you an example from my personal dream journal.

I dreamt I was trying to lock a tiger out of my house. I got the bolt to the front door in place and stood, I hoped safely, just inside. The tiger was in the yard, looking around, almost curiously. It was not running angrily toward me or baring threatening teeth. It did come up to the door, and stop, as though it were trying to look in. It seemed mildly surprised, almost disappointed, then turned around and wandered off into the woods.

The tiger was apparently a symbol of something going on in my personal/ domestic life, since it was in my front yard. I did not want to let it, or whatever it symbolized, in, although I recognized it was not an immediate threat. So what, I asked myself, do tigers mean to me, and exactly what is going on in my life?

I think of tigers as big, beautiful, powerful cats. They live in a jungle environment, which is warm, colorful, and filled with exotic animals and flowers. At the time there was a popular commercial by a gasoline company, which advised the listener to "put a tiger in your tank" by filling up with its brand. This would apparently give your car engine the best "energy" available. "Tony the Tiger" was also touting frosted cornflakes, which apparently gave Tony all sorts of delicious vitamins and thus the energy he needed.

Now, what was going on in my life? I was writing a book. I was dragging my feet. I wasn't using my resources. I was doing just enough every day to kid myself that I was moving ahead.

So, I asked my tiger to tell me what the deal was.

He spoke right up. "I just wanted to take you for a ride into the jungle, to have a good time, a real adventure. I didn't want to hurt you. I thought it would be fun."

I was amazed, but no longer in the dark. The tiger was a part of me, waiting to be experienced. I needed to be bolder, to grasp that great pool of energy that was waiting to be used, to put more of myself into my project, and to have a good time with it. I needed to combine the exotic and the domestic into a melting pot of creativity. I needed to take a ride on the wild side – and soon. The amazing thing was that this "jungle" was right outside my own front door, and I had my own tiger to give me a ride. I was doing myself a disservice by trying to lock it out.

My book was published a few months later.

CREATE A DIFFERENT ENDING

"Though no one can go back and make a brand new start, anyone can start from now and make a brand new ending." Author Unknown.

You sink into sleep, in your dark, quiet bedroom, pulling your cozy sky-blue blanket up around your neck. Soon you are dreaming ...

You are wandering around at night in the parking lot of a hotel, looking for your car. You are anxious to get home, but search as you might, you cannot find that car. You look in the area closest to your room, in the handicapped spot, in the adjacent lot, in the employee's parking lot – it is nowhere. You search your memory. Where did you park? Where did you enter the hotel? How did you get to your room? No answers come. You awake frustrated and a bit fearful. What can this mean? You always remember where you park in real life!

Your immediately enter the dream in your journal.

Analyzing your dream, you determine that your car represents your mobile self, the self you present to the world as you travel about. You are at a hotel, so the environment of the dream suggests that this dream commentary is not about your domestic life, but about your business or social endeavors. You do travel for your employer from time to time, as well as for pleasure, usually staying in hotels.

You do not always feel comfortable away from home and feel you have to put on a different face for clients and sometimes for friends as well. You wish you could mesh your private and personal self and become more comfortable in the public arena. You are "in the dark" as to how to do this, however. Who and where is the "real" you?

You decide to title your dream. You choose "Searching."

Ok. You have taken all the usual steps suggested for dream work. You have confronted your dilemma. You are, however, still a bit at sea. Is there another tool to use? One good technique is to create a different ending for your dream.

In this case, you might decide to go back into the hotel and get some help. You may ask the manager of the hotel to turn on the floodlights for the parking lot. You might ask a friend, a hotel employee, or even a stranger, to get a flashlight and come out with you to help find your car. You might call your sister and have her come and get you, intending to come back later to find your car.

These would all be possible scenarios that would help you find your car, sooner or later. You realize as you construct this ending that you have to ask for help and that you need some light shed on the subject parking lot. You can't just leave yourself parked out in the dark in the middle of nowhere.

You decide to take some action. You're not sure what that will be. You might consult a counselor, read a self-help book, or just talk to your sister. But you are determined to find your real self and be comfortable with it. Good going.

RE-ENACT A DREAM SCENE
"Action is the foundational key to all success." Pablo Picasso.

Let's drop in on Ann, who is contemplating her most recent dream.

Wow, what a dream. Let me get that on paper before I have another thought. Let's see, I was at a large table and there was nothing but apples on it! Red, green, yellow; large, small, in between; in bowls, on plates, atop placemats. What in the world could that mean? Well, while I'm waiting and cogitating, I'll just show the universe that I'm serious about this dream interpretation business. I'll eat an apple!

Now it's down to business. I've got to get this vacuuming done… I wonder how daughter Susie's doing; she's the apple of my eye – wait, apple? Hmmm. My children and grandchildren are the apples of my eye, and they are quite diverse. They come in many sizes, shapes, and colors, but they're all beautiful to me. I really should appreciate them each for their special individuality and stop worrying. Thanks, Universe.

Ann had decided to take her dream literally, to get things going, by eating an apple. This often works wonders. It jogs recognition of the symbol used and leads to understanding. If by chance the dream actually means to eat more apples, well, you're ahead of the game.

SHARING DREAMS WITH A GROUP
"None of us is as smart as all of us." Ken Blanchard.

Sometimes the answer just won't come. What then?

Dream Workshop Groups
You've decided dreams are important. You've worked on germinating dreams, remembering dreams, recording dreams, deciphering dream symbols, interpreting dreams, and acting upon dreams. Whew. What next?

Now that you feel confident and know your own symbols, it's time to branch out. Dream groups are fun and stretch your mind. You meet people with like goals and mindsets. You can do some great dream brainstorming.

Usually these groups meet once a month for about two hours. It's best to keep a group small (4-6 dreamers is ideal) so that everyone has the chance to present a dream. You bring your dream journal and choose one of your most perplexing dreams, one that has stayed with you and gnawed at your mind. The group works on it together, each person giving his/her suggestions until one of them hits you with a big 'aha'.

When presenting your dream, give details as though the listener is from Mars and knows nothing about your world, not even what a piece of paper or a banana is, or who Elvis was. This allows for rich detail without pre-conceived notions obscuring interpretation. (Even when working on your own, this is good advice.) For example, you might say, "I saw a piece of fruit which had a solid outer peel, yellow in color; it had a curved shape. I had to remove the peel to get to the inner soft sweet meat." Doesn't that provide a better clue to what's going on than, "I saw a banana."?

It's amazing how someone from the outside often gets the drift of your dream immediately. In fact, without knowing it, you may be resisting the message your dream is trying to deliver. You may not like what it says, or what it indicates you have to do to resolve a dilemma. On the other hand, you may just be blocked, looking at the dream from the wrong angle, or not connecting it with the relevant event in your life.

You do have to check your ego at the door. Everyone must be able to inquire, and to remain open, so that the heart of the dream can be exposed. You don't have to explain what your 'aha' moment has brought you, if it is extremely personal, but most of the time it is nice for group rapport to let your dream friends know how their input has helped.

An added bonus of dream sharing is that another's dream can sometimes be of help to you personally. You may be in the grips of a situation similar to that of your co-dreamer. As the group unravels your friend's dream, it may also give *you* that 'aha' moment of understanding just as though the dream were your own.

Dream groups can also dream for each other! Let's say Mary is having a hard time with a particular issue and asks for help. The other members agree to incubate a dream to address their friend's problem. Before going to sleep, you ask for a dream that will give light to Mary's quest for resolution. It often happens that each member of the group will have a dream contribution; putting all these together resolves the issue. It's like a dream jigsaw puzzle. This is possible because such groups become close, and the members become in tune with each other, sharing personal energy on a regular basis. You subconsciously pick up bits and pieces of information which you store away until needed.

The only caution with groups is that you must feel comfortable. Everyone needs to be on the same page and have the same goals. If you don't feel quite right, or the group gets too 'social' when you still need help with your dreams, don't hesitate to find another group, or even start one up yourself. It's somewhat like choosing a counselor or a doctor. It must fulfill your personal needs. Once you have the right group, however, there's nothing like it for an exciting adventure toward personal growth.

Intuitive Support Groups
These dream groups work with a slightly different focus.

One member provides a Guided Meditation, inducing a relaxed, semi-trance state. The dreamer then narrates his dream. At various points, the guide may stop the dreamer, asking the group to share any thoughts, feelings, impressions, colors, or images they have received. Has a title suggested itself? The dreamer then continues describing his dream to its completion. The trance state is terminated, and all members share their thoughts and perceptions.

This group works through collective energy. You are given the opportunity to get to depths that may not be possible one-on-one. In the group mind, one individual may receive a slice of understanding, which triggers an intuitive hunch from another member, which takes a third member to yet a deeper level. The pieces eventually fit together to form a composite, overall picture.

If you are more intuitive than cognitive, this type of group might fit your needs quite well. The practical considerations of size and comfort level still apply. Whatever works for you is what is right for you.

Family Dream Groups

Once you've tried working with your dreams in whatever mode you choose and feel comfortable with your skills, you may want to introduce your family to your fascinating studies. Try sharing dreams around your kitchen table. You will discover everyone has a dream or two to relate. This helps your children realize the potential, the fun, and the importance of dreams. I suggest keeping it very simple at first, so the young ones don't feel overwhelmed. To your surprise, they may soon be giving you a tip or two!

Let's look at a few examples of group dream work.

Avoiding That Interpretation?

"Your heart knows your song, but you have to be willing to listen to the words." Sue Rock.

You are usually quick to get at least a glimmer of your message. At times, however, you are just plain stymied. "What in the world can this mean?" you ask. This may be a good time to go to your dream group for help.

Patsy brought just such a dream to her group. The group knew that Patsy's teenage son was having problems with depression. In Patsy's dream, she was sweeping the living room floor with a small broom. She would then lift a corner of the rose-colored rug and sweep all the dirt right under the rug. The rug soon became lumpy and bumpy. Patsy was puzzled. She wasn't a bad housekeeper. Her rug was blue, not rose – and she had a much larger broom.

The group went to work. The dream was domestic, since it took place in her home, and probably focused on the family since it was in a general area of use, the living room. The rug was rose, which is a color that many associate with love (or with rose-colored glasses). The broom, being small, was inadequate for the job, but Patsy still managed to sweep with it, depositing all the 'dirt' under the rug. It was suggested that perhaps Patsy was hoping that her love for her son would be a cure-all, would cover all his problems and make them go away. However, they couldn't be hidden, but kept surfacing. Patsy needed a bigger broom, a professional, to get the task done.

Patsy didn't like the message, but it did seem obvious. She was surprised she hadn't recognized it right away. Normally, it would have been a piece of cake. She knew she had been avoiding the conclusion, because it was hard to admit that it would take more than a mother's love to help her son. She did take the dream's revelation to heart, however, and got her son to a counselor.

This was a good session and a good solution. It doesn't always work that way. A dreamer may acknowledge both his dream and the message. He decides, however, that the dream must be about someone else. It can't possibly be about him. Such a dreamer puts a cloth over the mirror and goes on his way. How sad.

Try very hard to look honestly into your own mirror. It only hurts for a little while. Remember, God prunes those he loves. And love us He does. Our dreams can help us rise above our weaknesses and turn them into strengths.

Blocking That Dream Out?
"Self is the only prison that can ever bind the soul." Henry Van Dyke, *The Prison and the Angel.*

The following scenario will sound familiar. Blocking and avoiding dreams are very similar. Blocking tunes them out completely. Avoidance is, hopefully, only temporary.

You have a dream that doesn't make any sense. You finally take it to your dream group. The group works hard, but you never get one of those "aha" moments that says, "This is It." You go away a bit frustrated.

But wait. Did you listen to *all* the suggestions? Or was there one tiny hint that passed you by, that you didn't home in on, that, in fact, you *avoided*? Perhaps you began talking loudly about another aspect of the dream just after a key remark was made. I will give you an example:

We peek into the life of Liz. She has been going through bad times for years now. She had breast cancer twice, now has MS, and her husband (just to prove things can get worse) recently had a bout with cancer himself. Liz craves love and attention and sympathy. She keeps up with her dream group, hoping they will supply some of her needs, along with providing dream interpretation, of course. She never fails to mention one or other of the symptoms of her illness. She moans and groans and cries. Everyone feels for her, but it is hard to feel but so bad for someone who is feeling sorry for herself with such élan. More sympathy seems almost extraneous. Added to this is the fact that she somehow "knows it all" – the group sometimes wonders why she even bothers.

Here is her written account of a "blocked" dream:

> I had such a puzzling dream. One of the few I just couldn't get. I even took it to my dream group, but they weren't much help. I was sitting at the head of a long table, one like at the group. Everyone was sitting around. In the middle of the table was a huge bowl full of wine bottles. There were other various healthy foods on the table, but the centerpiece was all this wine. I heard someone mention a play on words, but didn't quite catch what that meant. Wine to me means a celebration, but I haven't had much to celebrate about lately.

You notice that the abundance of wine was at the center of the table. It dominated the table, almost overwhelming the presence of other offerings. The comment made by a group member about a play on words was that "wine" might actually be translated to "whine". Of course, this comment was not heard by the dreamer. It was blocked. Liz was not ready to see the reality of how her negative attitude was taking over, becoming the center of her life, crowding out helpful spiritual, physical, and mental sustenance that was available.

Poor Liz was going to get the same result as if she had never put her dream down on paper.

PRAYER
"The value of consistent prayer is not that He will hear us, but that we will hear Him." William McGill.

Another way to untangle a problem can be to ask the Universe for guidance.

Amy's diary details the following life experience, resolved for her by a dream, one sent after an earnest prayer:

I have been praying for my troubled child for so long. Why is nothing happening? God says to have faith, but it is hard when I see no results time after time. I have been learning about dreams and their wisdom, so perhaps I should pray for a dream. I might understand a visual message better than the waking signs I am probably missing.

I go to bed early, read my favorite passage from the Bible about the prodigal son, and pray for a dream. My pen and paper are ready...

As I awaken, I am at peace and sense a deep patience I have never felt before. I immediately begin to write. The dream flows into my consciousness. I see a white light coming toward me, and a voice comes from within the light. It tells me, in a most loving tone, "Seek, yes. Then wait for God's time and God's answer." There then appears a strange clock, floating in space, with no hands.

I continue to pray for my child, but no longer feel a sense of urgency. I end my prayer with, "Thy Will be done," and I gladly leave the results with Him, who knows all. I give my child my love and my time and wait for God's time for the rest.

Sometimes visual messages, like the light and the clock in Amy's dream, can make all the difference. Don't hesitate to ask for a helpful dream when you are feeling lost and at sea.

WHAT ABOUT A DREAM DICTIONARY?
"The road to success is dotted with many tempting parking places."
Author Unknown.

What, you may ask, is a Dream Dictionary?

A dream dictionary is a compilation of symbols that frequent many dreams, with suggestions about the meaning of said symbols. What a dream dictionary is *not* is an even more important question.

Dream Dictionary No-No's

We all want it quick, cheap, and easy. I call it the McDonald's mentality. Let's see how far that gets us:

Diana awakens with a start. She muses: "Oh, my God, I had the strangest dream. I was dancing with a bear! Whatever can that mean?"

"I know, I'll check my 'Dedli Dream Dictionary'. It will tell me everything. Hmm, it seems to say I want to join the circus. Since I'm 46, can't dance, and know no bears, I sincerely doubt this could be true, but that's what it says."

Unfortunately, Diana doesn't go any further. She doesn't ask herself, "What do bears mean to *me*?"

Let's create a different scenario:

Diana awakes with a start. She reviews her dream. However, Diana doesn't have a 'Dedli Dream Dictionary', so she has to think things out herself.

She ponders her bear. She realizes that she thinks of a bear as wild but also as an animal that can be tamed and might even be fun. A bear, however, always really remains a bit wild and is thus risky to play with.

She goes one step more and asks herself if there is anyone in her life who resembles this bear, or if she herself resembles that bear. She comes to the conclusion that her current boyfriend, with whom she enjoys dancing, is a lot of fun but is still a bit wild. She considers whether or not she can accept the risk/reward of wild/fun, and what her expectations are. Does she want to dance exclusively with Mr. Bear?

Dream dictionaries have always been popular. They date back at least to "A Treatise of the Interpretation of Dreams" published in 1601. Your best bet – be your own Dream Dictionary. You know yourself, and your symbols, better than anyone else.

Down the road, if you've worked as hard as you can, solicited the input of friends and family, and still gotten nowhere, you might take a peek at a dream dictionary to see if it gives you a helpful boost. Don't, however, let it pre-empt your brain. If the interpretation suggested doesn't seem to fit, it probably isn't right, even if it is in a dream dictionary.

Remember, too, that there are multiple types of dream dictionaries. If you must have one on hand, choose one that is in sync with your mindset, goals, beliefs, and ideals. They are not all alike!

I know many will succumb to temptation. I have therefore appended a partial dream dictionary at the end of this chapter, for use when you become desperate. I have tried to include a variety of interpretations, but remember, in the end, it's up to you and you alone.

IT'S TIME TO ACT
"If you want to make your dreams come true, the first thing you have to do is wake up." J.M. Power.

After identifying events and emotions from your life that may have inspired a dream, decide how to deal with them in the future. Imagine a new ending that works for you. Ask if it is healthy, appropriate, and practical. These questions will tell you if the advice you gleaned from the dream is worth following (and if it was what the dream really meant). All that's left is to apply what you've learned.

Dream Dictionary

WARNING:

Not advised for use until you have worked with your dreams for at least six months and established your own personal dream symbols. Then use sparingly, and only when you are completely stymied.

<u>Beware</u>: The meaning of your symbol might not be as defined here. Dreams are always perfectly molded to the individual dreamer. Symbols don't exist in a vacuum.

Now, before you take a peek, do a quick review. Have you taken into account your current life, life changes, life challenges, friends, family, goals? Did you review the chapter on Interpretation? Are there any techniques you may have missed?

Then, if you must, peruse these suggestions. Keep an open mind. If you get an 'aha' -great. If not, check back with your dream group or dream guru. You want the meaning that is yours and yours alone.

★★★

Angel - Guardian Angel; safety, protection, wisdom; guidance; a messenger; upcoming birth or death.

Angry - Yelling at someone? Is it yourself? Just getting it off your chest? (Take note of your feelings/actions and the characteristics of the person or environment at which you are upset.)

Animals - A part of yourself, or someone in your life, based upon your analysis of the qualities, and your feelings about, that particular animal.

> Attacked by an Animal - 'wild' impulses or emotions that you find threatening, either within yourself or as displayed by others. (Note: What qualities do you associate with the animal? Does it remind you of part of yourself, of someone else you know, or of a conflict going on in your life?)

Arrow - A coming message; love-struck ('Cupid's arrow'); vengeance; bull's eye; right on the mark; a hunting weapon needing eye/hand coordination and strength.

Baby - A new venture or new relationship; innocence; something which appears to be small but may be of the greatest value; undeveloped, immature, childish; just getting started; free of responsibilities; something or someone needing nurturing and encouragement.

Bath - Cleansing (inner or outer) from old ideas; submerging yourself in cleansing; domestic emotions.

Bear - Two sides, one wild, the other playful; grumpy; overprotective; falling stock prices ('bear market'); hibernating, retreating; teddy bear; papa bear; play on words – 'bare'.

Bed - Sexual activity; intimacy; rest or sleep; unconsciousness; dream environment.

Bird - Messenger; freedom; flying high; the soul; aspirations; nester; eats worms; chirps, sings; lays eggs.

> Specific birds: The dove may symbolize gentleness and spirituality, or a good message (Noah and the Ark); the raven and crow are usually darker symbols;

the eagle is noble and ruthless; the peacock, beautiful but self-absorbed. (Note: If you were traumatized by Hitchcock's "The Birds" you may not feel too comfy-cozy about birds. If you have had bird droppings splat in your hair, you may not think too kindly of them either. Always seek your own take on things.)

Blanket, quilt, bed cover - Cover-up; comment on domestic life. (Note: notice color and pattern).

Boat - The voyage of life; a forthcoming trip; a message about spiritual truth; ferryboat separating from a pier – a voyage into the afterlife; having challenges in common with others in the boat ('we're all in the same boat'); an adventure; an opportunity ('don't miss the boat').

Body - The head symbolizes thought and identity; you may be 'ahead' of yourself; the face represents the personal image you present to the outside world; acne or blemishes on the face may mean you're feeling guilty, or unclean, about something; if you can't see your face, you could be unwilling to recognize some aspect of yourself.

Book - Knowledge; lessons gained; memories; ideas (Note: setting, color, and type of book are factors).

Box - Holds and protects memories and keepsakes; 'boxed in'; a present; a surprise.

Bread - A fundamental food; used in a sandwich (do you feel 'sandwiched in'); are you toasting the bread (feeling 'toasted'); play on words: 'that's toast'.

Bull - Stubbornness (bull-headed); bull market; sexual appetite.

Bull's eye - On the mark, right on; you have a winner.

Burglar - A warning that someone may take advantage of you; a negative attitude that is stealing your energy; guilt about having taken something from someone; desire to take something from someone (power, prestige, etc.).

Butterflies - Natural development and change; transformation.

Cake - Something luxurious or not practical; reward; celebration; play on words: easy, as in 'it's a piece of cake'; warning, as in 'you can't have your cake and eat it too'; insensitive, as 'let them eat cake'.

Candle - Your personal light; physical resources ('burning a candle at both ends'); enlightenment, wisdom; encouragement ('don't hide your light under a bushel'); birthday.

Car - The vehicle (body) by which you move through life; speeding car – hurrying or forcing an issue; the type and color of the car may show your current emotions or desires, your status or social standing; trouble with the brakes – lack of self control; who is driving – are you or someone else in control? Look for plays on words related to make or model (a Cougar, Accent, Chrysler ('Christ-ler'), Mustang, Ranger, etc.).

Cat - Independent; aloof; gossipy, "catty"; sexuality; kitten – prankster, playful.

Chased - Running from part of yourself, or from a situation or person, which frightens you.
> Unable to run - Paralyzed; unable to take meaningful action; stuck in life; you do not want to run.

Childhood home - Memories; old baggage; (Ask: At what age did you live there? What were your feelings? What is the scenario? Does it relate to your present life? How?

Children - Hope; simplicity; innocence; vulnerability; needing care; those who ask and seek to learn; a wish to return to childhood; unrealized potential; new ideas; activity or project that is as old as the child in the dream; childishness or immaturity in yourself or another.

Church - Spiritual messages related to both your daily life and your inner journey.

Clothing - Outer personality; attitudes and behavior; your occupation/the vocational role you assume; the persona shown to the world; the way you appear to others; protection from elements and the outside world.

Coat - Protective thoughts and attitudes (the color and type of coat will be a clue);
        Raincoat – protection from emotional upset.

Colors –
        Black - obstructions; ignorance; mystery; unconscious
        Blue - truth; spiritual feelings; calm, contemplative, peaceful; healing
        Golden - truth for the mind; something valuable; powers of the soul
        Green - development, growth; nature; receptiveness; envy
        Orange - Intuitive, tactful, diplomatic, cooperative; an orange
        Pink - love, innocence, health (in the pink)
        Purple spirituality, royalty, leadership

Red - love; energy; blood; passion; anger; physical desire; need to stop (as in 'stop sign')
White - purity; innocence; oneness
Yellow - Mental, creative, full of light (enlightenment)

Death - Letting go of the old, to prepare room for the new; loss of a talent; coming challenges; the equalizer, which brings all people to one level; the loss of a trait which is a characteristic of the person who has died; the need for sending prayers for and love to the one who has died; transition or change.

Deceased Person - 1) an actual visitation from a loved one, to communicate with you, to help you, or to ask for help from you; 2) a symbol connected with the personality or qualities of the deceased person, whether a loved one, or an historical figure.

Dirt/dirty - A part of you that needs to be cleaned up ('clean up your act'); warning to avoid any appearance of questionable moral conduct.

Diving - You want to discover your deeper feelings about a situation; you are taking immediate action (diving right in).

Dog - Trust/lack of; faithful/not; friend/enemy; things 'going to the dogs'; aggressiveness; obedience. (Note: What kind of dog is this, what is the dog doing, where is the dog, what attitude do you have toward dogs?)

Door/doorway - Opening to an opportunity, or to the outside world; locking the back door – wanting to avoid unpleasant conditions; front door –meeting new life experiences; closing doors – opportunities that are shut off; death.

Dress - Your appearance in the eyes of others; the self-image you have adopted; a new dress indicates new thoughts, ideas or projects.

Dying or being killed - This is usually a red flag – something in your life is going wrong, or needs changing. Who is killing you? Is it yourself, or someone else? Analyze the action, persons, and environment.

> <u>Another person dying</u>. - Your relationship with that person may be dying; you may be afraid of that person leaving you, even for just a short time.

Electric power line - The energy that allows things to get done – it may be coming from a long distance.

Elevator - Changes, ups and downs; altered states of consciousness; meditation.

Enemies - Relationships; parts of you that you are in denial about; a warning about someone who is not what he/she seems to be.

Explosion - Turmoil, anger, frustration.

Eyes - Your outlook or vision; large eyes – an all-seeing vision of things; intelligence; curiosity; personal identity; if damaged, have your eyes checked. Plays on words: 'I'; 'I've got my eye on you'.

Can't see through a window because of mist or dirt on the panes? You may be having difficulty seeing the truth about a situation; this also applies if you dream you are blind. It could also mean you need to have your eyes examined. Get your eyes examined, just in case.

Falling - Worry about failing in a real-life situation ('falling down on the job'); loss of balance; lack of support; not in control; being helpless and in an emotional free fall; dangerous, sometimes self-destructive behaviors; getting caught up in something ('falling in love'); in danger of losing social status or emotional security ('a fall from grace'); unethical or immoral behavior on your part ('a fallen woman'); may signal depression; fear of flying in an airplane. There may also be a literal meaning that warns of a hazardous condition, such as an unsafe railing on a balcony.

Fence - Confined by your own limited vision; hedged in; undecided ('sitting on the fence'); barrier; difficulty with expression; protection from outside threat; wanting freedom ('don't fence me in').

Fire - Anger; cleansing; warmth; civilization; campfire – warmth of friends; emotions raging out of control (forest fire); transformation or change; fevers or diseases (see a doctor if at all unsure).

Flower - Hope; beauty; love; growth; you are about to blossom.

Flying - Overcoming physical laws; awakening to a higher understanding; upcoming travel; desire to avoid something; desire to rise above things; idealism; fantasy or wishful thinking.

> <u>Pleasant flying dreams</u>. Free of inhibitions; soaring with a greater sense of individuality and dedication; going upward without constraint or tension, and down without gravity(!); not earthbound; Questions: Need to make a breakthrough? Get free, to soar and fly? How do you feel about all this flying? Are you perhaps showing off?
>
> <u>Unpleasant flying dreams</u>. Unable to get off the ground; tangled up with high *tension* wires; feel stuck; can't take off; can't stay 'up'; running away (using flight as an escape).

Food - That which nourishes; in a health dream, it might indicate you need to eat more of a particular food, or need the vitamins/ minerals in that food; if negative, it may indicate foods you should avoid (Note: be aware of setting, mood, emotions); Play on words – 'starved for love'.

> Hungry - not well nourished, either physically, or emotionally.
> Hearty meal or feast - emotionally or physically well-nourished.
> Sharing a meal - you feel close to that person (are fed by the same likes/dislikes, have common interests).

Friend - Compare this person's traits and personality with yourself, those close to you, or your present life circumstances.

Glasses - Enhanced comprehension; clear sightedness; mind-set ('rose colored glasses'); something which aids inner vision; need to get your eyes checked (see an optometrist).

Hair - Thoughts; strength (Note: Is the hair long or short, curly or straight; what color?)

Hands - Do you have a 'handle' on things; can you 'handle' the situation; are you offering a 'helping hand'; an injured hand could show loss of control; great dexterity shows you have the confidence to tackle a dream (or job) and solve it.

House - Domestic life; your body; your personality; front of house – the façade shown to the world; basement – subconscious or instincts; attic – memory; roof – intellect; individual rooms – stages you've passed through; old house – past, memories; spiritual home.

> Condition - Is the house in need of repair? Tidy? Snug? Spacious and airy?
> Discovering new rooms - Discovery of new parts of yourself, new potentials, new areas to explore.

Horse - A messenger; a part of you or someone in your life – a clue may be found in the kind of horse (charger, slow workhorse, race horse, pony); making progress; unbridled emotions; being caught up in a horse race; on a race track – running around in circles; strong as a horse; may be a sex symbol.

Intruder - If the intruder breaks into your home, you may have broken a domestic or spiritual law; the threatening and avoided side of yourself, or someone in your life; something/someone robbing you of part of yourself.

Key - Knowledge or access thereto; safety; solution to a problem; locking or keeping things out, or in; play on words: a 'key' item.

Killed - See "Dying".

Lake - Peace and tranquility; a haven; reflects surroundings; emotions. (Note: is it a deep lake, shallow lake, are you afraid, are you engrossed with its beauty?)

Lost - Feeling lost in an emotional sense in your everyday life; having no sense of direction regarding a career or purpose in life; lost in a spiritual sense; feeling alone without the ability to form meaningful interpersonal relationships; (Note: Look for clues as to why you are lost and for how to make constructive changes.)

Luggage - Things you have at hand in your life; burdens, psychological or physical; life's trash; things you carry with you and need, or think you need; things you need for a journey.

Mask - Are you (or is someone you know) hiding your true thoughts or feelings?

Mirror - How you are seen by others; how you see yourself; self-examination; self-reflection, self-consciousness; narcissism; illusion, that which isn't real but only a reflection.

Missing a train, plane, boat or bus - Lost opportunity; frustration; an overscheduled life with so many deadlines you are missing the opportunity to be happy; (Note: Do you often think you have more time than you actually do? Then realize there is a deadline fast approaching?)

Money - Benefit or returns from efforts; sign of appreciation for services rendered; a way of indicating success, power, authority; time and/or energy.

> Counterfeit money - phoniness, cheating, insincerity.
> Finding money - Discovery of new and positive qualities and potential within yourself.

Naked - Exposure of something kept hidden; feeling exposed to criticism with no defense; vulnerable; stripped of the masks you wear in relating to the world; a desire for others to know your real feelings; the refusal to keep playing a role in life; lack of preparation; embarrassment − 'all laid bare'.

> Naked in public - Anxiety or worry about feeling overexposed; if onlookers are indifferent, you feel the world doesn't really notice your worries.
> Setting - Work, home, someplace else? What does clothing represent for you in that setting?

Numbers -

> One − Independent, original, a leader
> Two − Cooperative, diplomatic, emotional
> Three − Creative, optimistic, charming
> Four − Hard working, patient, dependable
> Five − Freedom loving, understanding, adventurous
> Six − Responsible, understanding, harmonious

Seven – Analytical, wise, spiritual
Eight – Efficient, successful, zealous
Nine – Charitable, compassionate, selfless

Objects - Ask what the object means to you. Why would a person have or use the object? How does it work?

Person - The person's traits and personality usually represent part of you, or part of someone in your current life.

Pregnant/Giving Birth - Working on or developing a new part of yourself; a new project is being developed; a new relationship is in the works.

Purse/Wallet - Your identity.
Losing your purse or wallet - Loss of identity or purpose in life, loss of power. Ask: Have you just retired? Entered a new phase of life? Have your kids left home? How do you feel about the loss? Is it just a big bother to replace everything? Can you live without it? Can you get a better one that suits your current needs?

Rain - Blessings; emotions and the release of feelings; sadness or grief; deliverance from a dry spell; something necessary for growth; a downpour may mean lots of problems; need to drink more water.

River - The journey of life; passage of time; source of fish.

Road/path/street - The journey of life you are on; rough, poor roadbed – troublesome conditions; junction, crossroad – choices in life; the direction you are going; your destiny; turning left, may be the past, right, the future; look for road signs.

Scales - Weighing something in your mind; making an important decision and considering the pros and cons; out of balance ('weighed and found wanting').

School - Lessons to learn; ability to teach others; unresolved issues from your school years; the desire to learn. (Note: is it an elementary school, high school, or university?)

Sex - A metaphor for feelings of intimacy, acceptance, rejection, domination; the person you are involved with in the dream may represent either a part of yourself or a caricature of someone you are currently involved with; obstacles often indicate the difficulties you are having in a current, intimate relationship.
> Sex with a celebrity? The qualities or habits you attach to that celebrity may represent a part of yourself or of someone in your life.

Shoes - Your understanding, or foundation; protection from rocky roads; a worn sole may be a warning that you need to repair your shoes (or what they represent). Play on words: to 'be in his shoes'; sole may refer to 'soul'.

Snake - Temptation; one who may harm in an underhanded manner; hissing – at yourself? shedding its skin – letting go of the past, getting a new identity; healing and wisdom (the serpent-entwined rod associated with the American medical association).

Spider - Warning about a threat (being caught in a web); the entrapping or smothering behavior of yourself or of others.

Stage - Something public; desire to be in the limelight; a stage of development; the center of your present attention or interest.

Teeth - Spoken words (sharp teeth point to sharp words or 'biting remarks'; a toothy smile may indicate you're too wordy); getting involved ('sinking your teeth into it'); effectiveness; eating, diet; see a dentist if at all unsure of your message.

> Falling out - loss of control, having no 'bite'; ineffective, feeble, helpless ('toothless'); fear of looking bad or losing face; something you said caused a loss.
> False teeth - a phony; if shiny, speech is only for show.

Telephone/Cell Phone - Means of gaining information or assistance; a coming message; communicating with others; telepathy; your own intuition. (Note: Communication is with one who is some distance away.)

> Phone does not work - Failure to communicate; need help with a situation; (Note: Ask: Who are you calling and why? Do you have good communication skills? Do you know who to call? Do you need better, more professional assistance, a better phone; need to contact yourself?) Do not ignore this type of dream.
> 911 - Help
> 411 - Information

Tests - Under a lot of pressure; being tested in your encounters with people in your career or private life; a need to be prepared; the need to know a certain subject well.

Toilets - Bathrooms provide privacy, time for just you; toilet bowl – a need to discharge emotions; putting something down the toilet – getting rid of that no longer needed, that which is unpleasant, or is wasteful.

> Trying to find a private toilet - may not want others to know about what you need to eliminate (are you in a dream group?).

Train - A train ride – the journey of life; a train of events; train tracks – the accepted way of doing things; an opportunity ('missed the train'); following the proper course (you're 'on track');

victimized, punished unfairly ('railroaded'); in training. Ask why you're on a train, rather than another mode of transportation.

Tree - Your individual self; your potential growth and rootedness in the world; an intermediary between your highest aspirations and your deepest roots.

Turtle - Longevity; methodical; introverted; tending to withdraw into a shell; encouragement to move slowly but surely (*The Tortoise and the Hare*).

Wall - An obstacle to be overcome before a goal can be attained; the moment of truth ('up against a wall') where you must do something that makes or breaks a situation; confinement; protection and shelter.

Water - Sea of life; cleansing; clearness of understanding, purity of purpose; emotions (calm, stormy, deep and clear?); need to drink more water. The location – pool, lake, river, ocean – will indicate the part of your life being addressed.

> <u>Dirty water</u> - imperfect understanding and knowledge.
> <u>Flood</u> - flooded with emotions, overwhelmed.

Wave - Conditions or people that are wavering; waves of emotion; being overwhelmed (a tidal wave).

Weather - Snow or ice, a chill in the air – being unloved; if you love winter and winter sports, you may be looking forward to a rush of adrenalin; hot weather – things are 'heating up'; sky dark, windy, stormy – unpleasant times being experienced, or on the way; spring is in the air – love, growth, sunny times ahead.

Woods/forest - A maze of trees where you can easily get lost or confused (*Hansel and Gretel*); the unconscious mind; a peaceful, natural place.

★★★

You have moved through the process. You believe in dreams, you remember your dreams, you faithfully record your dreams. You work hard on interpretation and have your symbols pretty much down pat. Next? Let's put those dreams to work so that they can *change your life.*

How to generate a specific dream for a specific purpose.

Mr. Dream Man, Bring Me A Dream . . .

"Help me if you can, I'm feeling down
And I do appreciate you being 'round.
Help me get my feet back on the ground.
Won't you please, please help me?" The Beatles.

You are desperate for a solution to a specific problem. You may be laboring with an invention, writing a story, or trying to perfect a recipe. Since you are now working diligently with your dreams, you decide to prod your dream world into giving you a clue.

Generating a specialized dream is a technique to use when you have already worked on a project, dilemma, or puzzle for a while, giving it the 'old college try.' The Universe doesn't want you to get lazy. Do your homework before you ask for a special favor.

When you're ready, try one of these basic techniques:

The Incubation Phrase
To use this technique choose a night when you are not too tired and have not had a nightcap or any medication which might affect your sleep. Review your dream journal; make note of the day's events. Have an internal discussion of the problem to be solved, thinking it through from every angle. Decide what needs to be

181

addressed and what kind of information would provide a working answer. Note any feelings associated with your predicament.

Next, come up with an *incubation phrase*, a one line question or request that provides a succinct description of the problem, showing a clear and deep understanding of the situation to be addressed. Focus on that phrase as you go to bed, clearing every other distracting thought out of your mind. Tell yourself, "I will remember my dream." On awakening, go through your usual recall and recording process, reviewing the information provided by the night's dreams for possible solutions.

Bill tried this technique when he was dying to go on a week's vacation with his family at a beach resort only a few hours away. He had been given an unexpected week off, due to a burst pipe and ensuing water damage at the office. He couldn't seem to find anything he could afford on such short notice. He did his prep work. He knew where he wanted to go and when, and what he could afford to pay. He knew he needed to book a place within two days. He chose the following incubation phrase, "I want to go to Rolling Waves Beach from August 20-27 and need a three bedroom cottage for under $800 for the week." During the night, he dreamed that he was talking to his friend Jay who lived just down the street. Jay was pointing to a crystal ball and showing Bill a beautiful place right on the beach.

The next morning Bill went over to see Jay and explained his problem. Jay was flabbergasted. He told Bill that his friend Crystal had just received a cancellation for a cottage she owned at the beach, and under the circumstances, Jay was sure she'd be glad to let Bill and his family have it for a good price. Off Bill and his family went on their 'dream' vacation. Aren't guardian angels, in and out of dreams, nice to have around?

The Pillow Note

Jean belongs to a dream group. She learned about a new technique in her last meeting, and is considering trying it out. Let's see what happens:

My dream facilitator said I could put a note under my pillow requesting a dream. I think it's pretty silly, but nothing ventured, nothing gained, right? At least it won't *hurt*. I can't seem to get along with my boss. Maybe I'll ask for tips in that department. I'll write, "I need help working with Grizzly Jones." Let's see what those dreams do for me now.

I can't believe it. I ask for help with my boss and I get a dream about flies – they're on my kitchen counter, all over the sugar that has spilled from my sugar bowl. I have to get the vinegar from the cupboard and pour it all over ... hey, wait a minute. Didn't my grandmother used to tell me you get more flies with sugar than with vinegar? I think I've been letting my sour attitude about my boss keep me from giving him compliments and really trying to get along. Hmmm. Maybe there is something to this dream stuff after all.

Jean tried the technique suggested by her dream. She now gets along quite well with her boss. She even admits to his having a few redeeming qualities.

Prayer

You are going through a difficult time. Your relationships are rocky. You don't feel in control. Peace eludes you. You know you must seek guidance, and fast.

You resolve to combine all of your super-human resources – prayer, meditation, and dreams. You are going for the best professional input available. The good news? It's all *free*.

You start with prayer, speaking with God, asking for enlightenment from the Universe. You meditate daily, quietly listening for the answers to your prayers. You now have the rapt attention of your higher sources, who will work overtime to get through. You have asked – they want to answer.

Answers often start with your dreams, giving you ideas, images, even spoken clues. Written messages are not unknown.

Your next nighttime dream presents a sign in the window of a pastry shop, advertising "Humble Pie". You then begin to have waking dreams. Three days in a row, you run into old friends whose egos have always been inflated. You start to connect the dots. "Hmmm, I wonder if I need to stop thinking only about myself," you conjecture. The thought that you might not always be right also filters into your mind.

Once you get that first breakthrough, things happen fast. More concrete suggestions come. You are browsing at the library when a book falls onto the floor. Don't put it back. Pick it up and look at it good and hard. It's undoubtedly one of those serendipitous gifts that the Universe has put right on your path. You note that the title is "A Flexible Universe." Later you run into a friend who starts talking about how he solved a particularly knotty problem. You find that his problem, and his solution, relate to your own situation.

Be alert and aware. There are no coincidences. Once you ask for help, you will get help. You just need to keep your eyes and ears wide open. Then act.

Read Me, Read Me!

"How many a man has dated a new era in his life from the reading of a book." Henry David Thoreau, *Walden*.

Struggling Sally muses about her lack of success with dreams. She joined a dream group to help jump start her progress but is still stymied. Her thoughts run thus:

I still haven't had any dreams, at least none that I remember. I've been so good – done my homework, moved the TV out of my bedroom. My dream journal is right on my nightstand. I've even put a note under my pillow asking for a dream about remembering dreams!

Well, maybe I'll read that dream book that was recommended at the seminar. I might get some inspiration from that.

Two weeks later…

Wow, after reading only two chapters, I'm having so many dreams I can't keep track. I start to write down one and remember two others. My hand gets cramps. Maybe I'll put a note under my pillow to restrict my dreams to two a night! I guess I finally convinced the universe I was serious. That book got me focused on dreams during the day, and bam – now I'm concentrating on them at night as well.

Sally, no longer struggling, finally had a dream to bring to her group. She was so proud. Her group applauded. She had kept on trying and found the key that worked for her.

If you find yourself in Sally's shoes, you might try a good book.

Got What You Wanted? Or did You?

You asked for help, and you awaken with a full-blown dream filling your mind. Do you reach for a pen? No, you jump out of bed, studiously avoiding your Dream Journal. You start vigorously attacking your chores for the day, running this way and that, putting all else out of your mind. You seem to have a frenetic need to expend your energy this morning on anything but writing down that dream. Why?

There are times when we just don't want to face our fears, our weaknesses, our call to action or change. We want to put it off, perhaps, in this case, hoping we will forget the dream! This will not help, I promise you. The Universe will not let up. You will continue to get that dream anyway, in bigger and better form, until you reach for that pen, write it down, and get busy on it.

It isn't always pleasant looking into our mirror. It's always helpful, however. We're never given more than we can bear. We usually get help in bite size pieces, so that we can work on ourselves and our lives at a pace that suits us. The Universe is very kind. However, if we ignore or avoid this help, we'll inevitably regret it. The helpful hints will get stronger, and we will find ourselves wallowing in our life's trash until we learn the hard way, if necessary. Write down that dream immediately, and the way won't be nearly as hard. Be strong. Be brave. You can do it.

Thank You!
When a gift is given to you, via a dream or other source, say "Thank You." This will encourage your angels to continue to work for you.

AT LAST
You are now a master of dream creation! You have solutions at your fingertips, all recorded in your very own dream journal. What comes next?

Well, it's time to put those dreams to good use.

Use your dreams to improve your life.

Follow Your Dreams

"Knowing is not enough; we must apply. Willing is not enough; we must do." Johann Wolfgang Von Goethe.

A dream is only as good as you make it. It can give you suggestions, insight, warnings, even tell you how to get rid of that ingrown toenail! If you don't take action, however, everything stays the same. You are left treading water.

Let's check out an ideal scenario. You identified what your dream was all about. You recognized challenges from your life and understood the message. You now must decide how to deal with the information and *plan a course of action.*

Remember the dream that screamed, "You're in the wrong field!" If you don't change the field in which you work after that dream, you deserve to be miserable.

You were there when poor Sarah got the message that her current boyfriend was just as jealous as a problem relationship in the past. Did she get stuck in his jealous clutches? Or did she move on?

Poor Millie knew her dream about dirty windows meant she should see her doctor. She didn't. A few years later, she had to have cataract surgery. What a shame.

Did you avoid the usual route to work when your dream predicted a big smash-up at the intersection you usually cross just before reaching the office? The dream showed your car scrunched like a tin can. I know you took a detour, since you're all in one piece.

The messages in these examples were all quite clear. Sometimes the message is a bit cloudy. In that case, you simply have to experiment. Did your dream feature an elephant? You decide to take your grandchildren to the zoo. If an elephant appears again in your dream, you might think about the phrase "an elephant never forgets." Perhaps you are holding onto old memories that are not helpful. You decide to work on forgiveness, and to live in the now.

There are dangers besides those immediately foretold in your dreams. Your body often gives you messages that are a bit more physical. Staying in a job that is not fulfilling your true potential may lead to ulcers, or a nervous breakdown. Staying in a relationship you know to be stressful can lead to headaches, of more than one kind. Not taking a detour – well, see you in the hospital!

Sometimes you may worry about following dream advice. You are afraid of change, or of taking action when everything seems to be going well already. Try it anyway! When you work with your dreams, the overall quality of your life improves. You will be able to play golf better, make better business decisions, make more money, be more alert to dangers for yourself and for those around you. Then too, as you use your dreams, you will receive even bigger and better dreams to follow up on. You have shown you are serious, and will reap the benefits.

"But," you might say, "I have responsibilities, duties, obligations. I can't just run off and become a movie star because my dream says I need to express my creativity on the stage." Well, that's probably true. But you can join the local community theater. One wife became an author and still maintained a secure home life; a sea captain became an environmental advocate, and stayed a good sea captain; a teacher became a prayer leader, and a better teacher; a mother became a psychic and stayed a good mother. Each of these people worked with their dreams for years. None of them flew off to Tibet.

Another benefit to using your dreams is that you begin to develop your natural intuition. You start to recognize in your waking life what you once had to be told in your dreams. You may know when a child is ill, how to approach your boss at work for that raise, or what is going to happen in the stock market. All this from using your dreams.

So toss off your fear and jump into the water with both feet. The least that will happen is that you get wet. You might also find hidden treasure, and bring it to the surface.

As you now know, dreams are real, dreams are personal, and dreams can change your life. You just have to let them!

"Somewhere over the rainbow, skies are blue, and the dreams that you dare to dream really do come true." Lyman Frank Baum.

Bibliography

Auerbach, Loyd. *Psychic Dreaming*. NY, NY: Warner Brothers, 1991.

Bell, Kaitlin. "5 Surprising Signs You're Sleep Deprived." *Prevention* Mar. 2010: 59.

Bro, Harmon H., PhD. *Edgar Cayce on Dreams*. NY, NY: Warner Books, 1968 by Association for Research and Enlightenment, Inc.

Burgess, Randy. *A Little Book of Dreams*. Kansas City: Ariel Books, Andrews and McMeel, 1996 by Armand Eisen.

Cayce, Edgar. *The Edgar Cayce Dream Dictionary*. Virginia Beach, VA: the Edgar Cayce Foundation, 1986.

Cayce, Hugh Lynn, et al. *Dreams the Language of the Unconscious*. Virginia Beach, Virginia: ARE Press, 1962, 1971, by the Edgar Cayce Foundation.

Chapman, Carole. *When We Were Gods*. Foster, VA: SunTopaz LLC, 2005.

Crook, Thomas, PhD. "Snooze It or Lose It." *Prevention* May 2008: 129.

Curtis, Patricia. "Sleep Like a Baby!" *Prevention* Jan. 2010: 63.

Daff, Ryan. "Gone Missing." *Ellery Queen* December 2009: 56.

Delaney, Gayle, PhD. *In Your Dreams*. NY, NY: San Francisco Harper, 1997.

Gelman, Lauren. "The Secret to Waking Up Happy." *Prevention* Nov. 2009: 18.

Goodwin, Doris Kearns. *Lyndon Johnson and the American Dream* NY, NY: St. Martins Press, 1976, 1991.

Greene, Gayle. "The Slumber Diaries." *Prevention* October 2008: 39.

Holden, Lee, LAC. "Get More Sleep, Energy & Sex." *Prevention* Nov. 2009: 134.

The Jerusalem Bible, Reader's Edition. Ed. Alexander Jones. Garden City, New York: Doubleday & Company, Inc., 1971.

Joseph, James, PhD. "Memory News You Won't Forget." *Prevention* Nov. 2009: 132-3

Kosecki, Danielle. "Play Up Your Brain Power." *Prevention* Oct. 2009: 107.

Murphy, Patricia, PhD. "Sleep Lab." *Prevention* Nov. 2009: 44.

Oz, Dr. Mehmet. "A New Bedtime Story." *Parade* 22 January 2012, 8-11.

Oz, Dr. Mehmet. "Get Back to Sleep." *AARP* Nov./Dec. 2010: 26.

Prevention Staff. "You Asked and Our 55 Experts Answered!" *Prevention* Nov. 2009: 133.

Redfield, James and Adrienne, Carol. *The Tenth Insight, Holding the Vision, AN EXPERIENTIAL GUIDE*. NY, NY: Warner Books, 1996.

Repinski, Karyn. "Now on Sale, Amazing Health." *Prevention* Nov. 2009: 58.

Rowing Team, The, LLC. "Top 7 Brain Benefits of Drinking Water." brain spade. 2012. 7/3/13 <http://brainspade.com>

Sandburg, Carl. *Abraham Lincoln: The Prairie Years & The War Years*. Pleasantville, New York: The Reader's Digest Association, 1970.

Svoboda, Elizabeth. "Dream up Better Health." *Prevention* Mar. 2009: 88-91.

Weil, Andrew, MD. "Aging Naturally." *Time* 17 Oct., 2005: 69.

Illustrations: www.thinkstockphotos.com

Front Cover: "Dreaming II" by artist Kristin Krahmer

Back Cover: Author photo by Sandra Colleen Elliott

Index

Alsop, Stewart, 14
Aristotle, 7
Bible, 9
Biblical dreams, 85
Blocked dreams, 102, 156
Caffeine, 109
Carbs, 110
Chinese, 8
Coleridge, Samuel Taylor, 17
Death, 39
Déjà vu, 83
Dream dictionary, 132,139,158,163
Dream groups, 151
Dream sequence, 130
Dream setting, 131
Dream symbols, 132,137
Dreams, defined, 1
Egypt, 8
ESP, 80
Exercise, 104,111
Falling, 44
Flying, 45
Freud, Sigmund, 9
Future revealed, 71
Generating a dream, 181
Greece, 7
Health dreams, 46
History of dreams, 7
Johnson, Lyndon B., 16

Journal, 117
Journal extras, 122, 123
Jung, Carl, 9
Lincoln, Abraham, 13
Lucid dreaming, 57
Mattress, 108
Medication, 112
Memory enhancement, 103
Memory-science, 43,102,104,117
Mesopotamia, 7
Mirrored dreams, 54
Multiple layer dreams, 28
Nicklaus, Jack, 15
Nightmares, 35
Past-life dreams, 75
People in dreams, 143
Percentages, 21
Persistent dreams, 121
Personal growth, 23
Physical influence, 22
Pillow note, 183
Prayer, 157,183
Promises, 34
Religious symbols, 133
Remembering dreams, 100
Repetitive dreams, 31
Self-revealing dreams, 24
Senoi, 8
Sex, 49

Shelley, Mary, 15
Sleep deprivation, 113
Sleep ritual, 111
Snoring, 114
Stevenson, Robert Louis, 17

TV, 106
Types of dreams, 21
Using dream information, 189
Visitations, 66

CPSIA information can be obtained at www.ICGtesting.com
Printed in the USA
BVOW07s1300171113

336439BV00001B/2/P

9 781452 583839